OF KNIVES
AND MEN

To Catherine, who has supported me in every sense of the word,
and who corrects my mistakes, even though it seems that I'm a hopeless case.

To Maxime, who is still not a knife enthusiast.

To Alexandre, who I miss terribly.

Acknowledgments:

To Gérard Leplé, collector and man of taste.

To Yves and Matthew Thomas.

To all writers, regular and occasional, at *La Passion des Couteaux* (Passion for Knives) magazine.

To all my friends and knife buddies, who practice a trade as old as time...
it's not always easy!

Published by Firefly Books Ltd. 2022
First published by Olo Editions,
www.oloeditions.com
© 2019, Éditions Gründ, a department of édi8, for the French edition.
© 2019, Olo Éditions, for all other editions.

First printing

Library of Congress Control Number: 2022936793

Library and Archives Canada Cataloguing in Publication
Title: Of knives and men / François-Xavier Salle.
Other titles: Couteaux et des hommes. English
Names: Salle, François-Xavier, author.
Description: Translation of: Des couteaux et des hommes. | Includes
    bibliographical references.
Identifiers: Canadiana 20220223467 | ISBN 9780228104001 (hardcover)
Subjects: LCSH: Knives—Design and construction—Pictorial works. | LCSH:
    Knives—Pictorial works. | LCSH: Knifesmiths. | LCGFT: Photobooks.
Classification: LCC TS380 .S2513 2022 | DDC 739.7/20222—dc23

Published in the United States by
Firefly Books (U.S.) Inc.
P.O. Box 1338, Ellicott Station
Buffalo, New York 14205

Published in Canada by
Firefly Books Ltd.
50 Staples Avenue, Unit 1
Richmond Hill, Ontario L4B 0A7

Editorial design: Nicolas Marçais
Artistic design: Philippe Marchand
Layout: Élise Godmuse and Thomas Hamel
Publishing: Nadja Belhadj
Editing: Ombeline Marchon
Translation: Travod International Ltd.

Printed in China

FRANÇOIS-XAVIER SALLE

OF KNIVES AND MEN

GREAT KNIFECRAFTERS OF THE WORLD AND THEIR WORKS

FIREFLY BOOKS

CONTENTS

Some prices may surprise you, but these are truly unique fine art knives:

- Under $500: *
- Between $500 and $2,500: **
- Between $2,500 and $6,000: ***
- Over $6,000: ***

The knife, an essential item which we have quite rightly named "man's first tool", no longer serves only to keep us alive. At the heart of all civilizations, it has endured the stone, bronze and steel ages to become a true collectors' item. It continues to evolve today thanks to new techniques and materials derived from the most advanced technology, aeronautics, and powder metallurgy. But, above all, thanks to new knifemakers, coming from all walks of life and from all continents, artisans, artists, creators and designers, who are giving this several-thousand-year-old craft a new beginning by making the knife an object more than ever of its time. The artisans chosen for this book are, in our eyes, the most representative of the last thirty years, each with their own style, which often reflects the traditional knifemaking traditions of their home country or culture. Since the dawn of time, man has decorated or embellished knives in order to personalize them, as shown in this photo by Yannick Kepinski (right) and this 19th century folk art knife, with a carved wooden handle (left).

The works featured in this book are worthy descendants, made by the best contemporary *custom* knifemakers. They are all truly unique pieces.

JULIAN ANTUNES

A young Brazilian blacksmith new to the world of knives, Julian already has the experience of a seasoned professional. Beneath his youthful looks, he knows how to do everything: the most complex Damascus steels, richly crafted integral knives, swords, daggers and Bowie knives.

His pieces make him feel as if he has made something that can be passed from generation to generation, and that brings him joy. He particularly likes the medieval and Renaissance styles, but when he's working, he draws inspiration from everywhere: "I see an interesting curve, a tiny detail in nature and an idea starts to form." He participates in the São Paulo Exhibition, BLADE Show Atlanta, and FICX-Paris. Julian accepts few orders and prefers to offer his work on the spur of the moment.

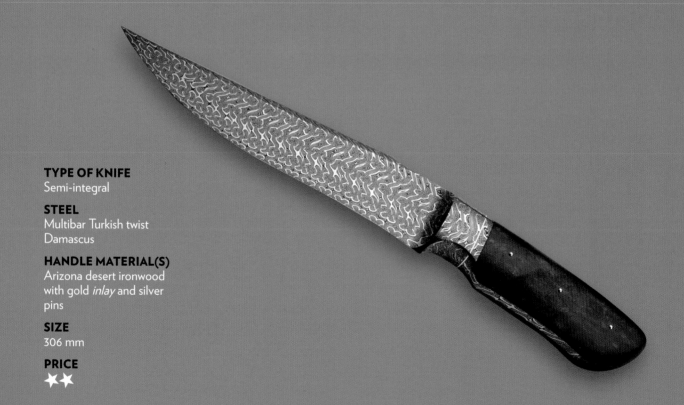

TYPE OF KNIFE
Semi-integral

STEEL
Multibar Turkish twist
Damascus

HANDLE MATERIAL(S)
Arizona desert ironwood
with gold *inlay* and silver
pins

SIZE
306 mm

PRICE
★★

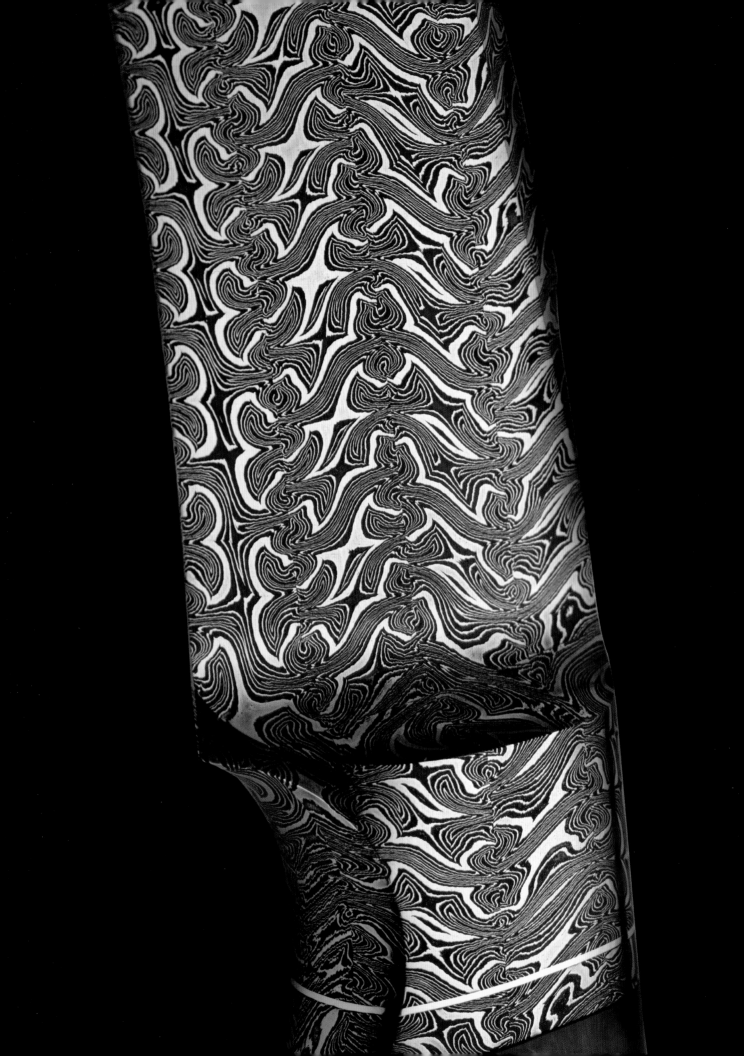

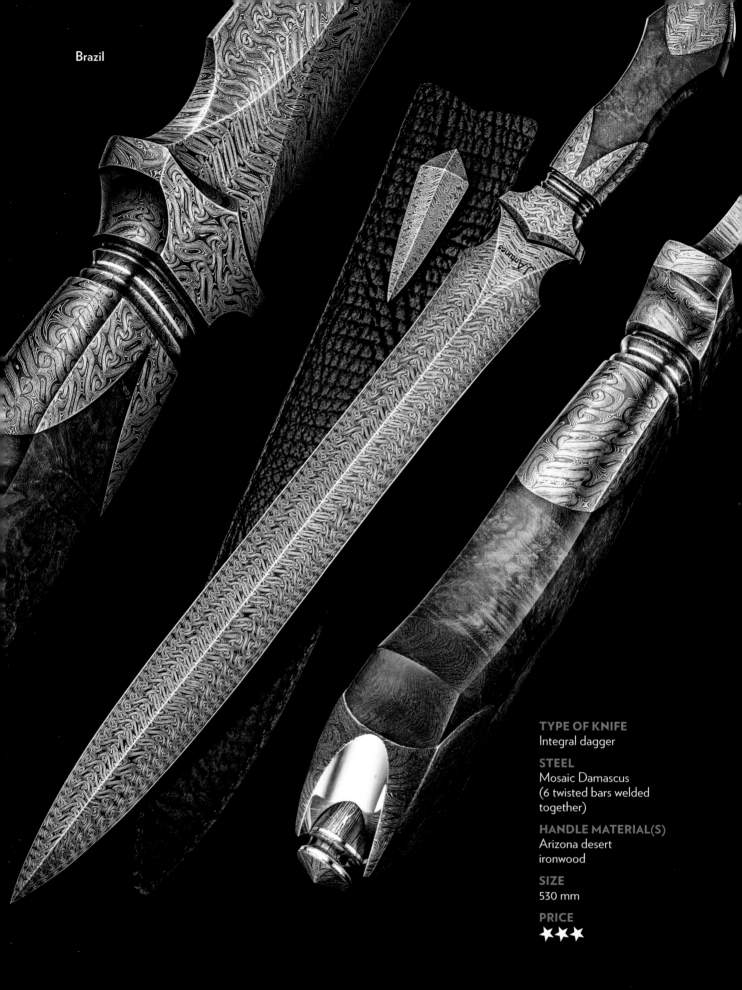

Brazil

TYPE OF KNIFE
Integral dagger

STEEL
Mosaic Damascus
(6 twisted bars welded
together)

HANDLE MATERIAL(S)
Arizona desert
ironwood

SIZE
530 mm

PRICE
★★★

TYPE OF KNIFE
Bowie

STEEL
Ladder Damascus

HANDLE MATERIAL(S)
Arizona desert
ironwood

PRICE
★★★

TYPE OF KNIFE
Bowie, can be fully
dismantled

STEEL
Mosaic Damascus

HANDLE MATERIAL(S)
Mammoth ivory

PRICE
★★★

ROBERT BEILLONNET

France's own *"Petit Robert"* was born in 1961, in the town of Châteldon, at the heart of Puy-de-Dôme in Auvergne, where the history of knifemaking is renowned. The town is also known for its high-quality mineral water. Affectionately known as "The Big Guy" — although he's not at all — he joined the famous *Maison des Couteliers* (Cutlery Museum) in Thiers as an apprentice, under the tutelage of Angel Navarro, in 1982. He moved on in the mid-nineties, when he became its director. He then worked in the Thiers knife manufacturing industry, but he quickly realized that he was not suited to mass production. He achieved his first award in the *"Un des Meilleurs Ouvriers de France"* (French Craftsperson of the Year) competition in 1997 and the second in 2000 — *MOF* and re-*MOF*, as it is printed on his business card. It was not until 2001 that he became a fine art knifemaker, to the delight of a wide variety of enthusiasts and collectors. His creations are varied, but his favorites are regional French knives, which are magnificent. Robert Beillonnet uses high-quality natural and artificial materials, sometimes using unusual combinations when he wants to get a reaction (always with a sense of humor). This is the case with his knives with scales made of "crate wood" or even stabilized cow dung — in response to the ban on the use of elephant ivory.

Robert Beillonnet mainly makes Yssingeaux, Issoire, Châtellerault, Laguiole, and Thiers folding knives, in one or more parts. He makes incredible Zeppelin knives, concealed knives, and particularly enjoys a challenge. His favorite material for blades is RWL-34 steel, or Damasteel©, a stainless Damascus steel. His initials (R.B.) on the knife blade are a mark of quality. Robert Beillonnet participates in the Coutellia show (Thiers), the *Fête du Couteau* (Knife Festival) in Nontron (Périgord) and FICX-Paris.

www.robert-beillonnet.com

TYPE OF KNIFE
Folding knife

LOCKING SYSTEM (FOR FOLDING KNIVES)
8-part Zeppelin

STEEL
RWL-34

HANDLE MATERIAL(S)
Ebony

PRICE

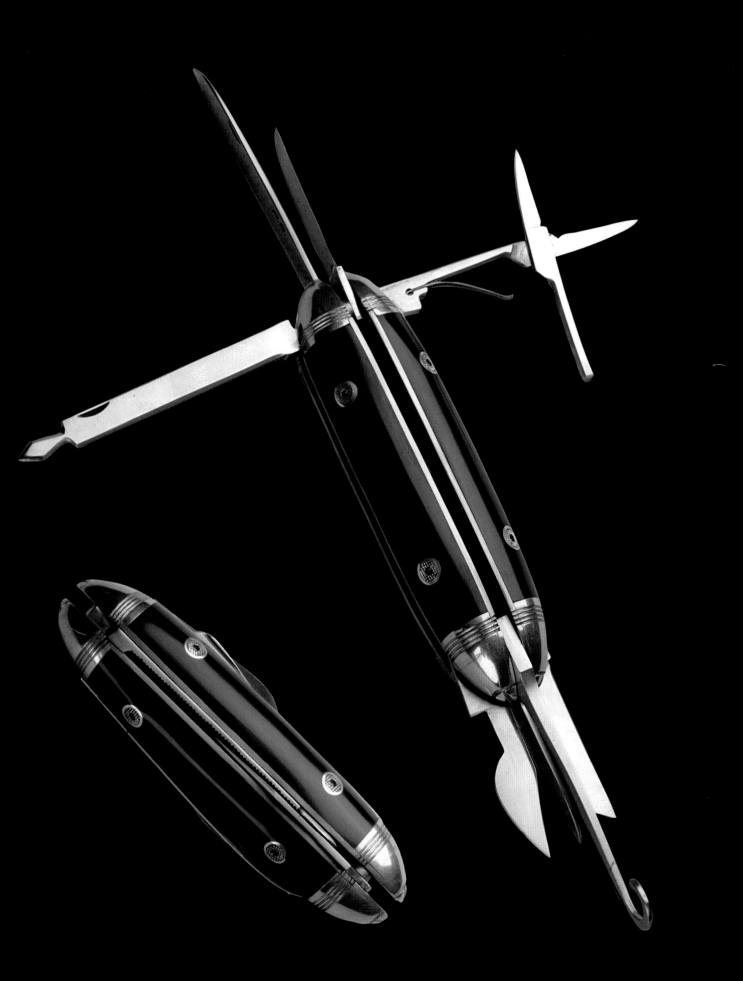

France

TYPE OF KNIFE
Châtellerault folding knife

LOCKING SYSTEM (FOR FOLDING KNIVES)
Pallet

STEEL
RWL-34

HANDLE MATERIAL(S)
Antique ivory

PRICE
★★

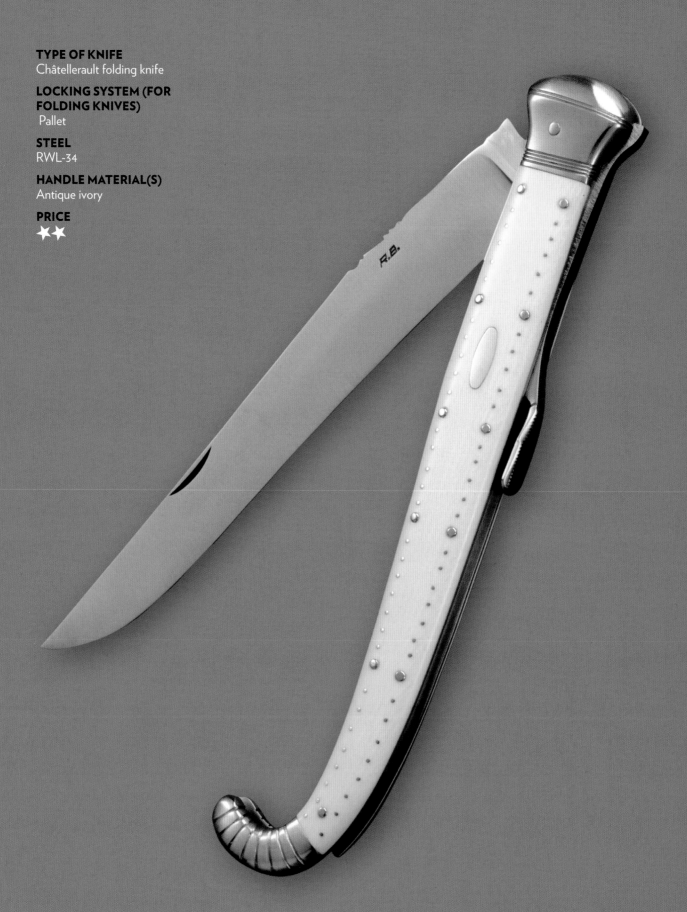

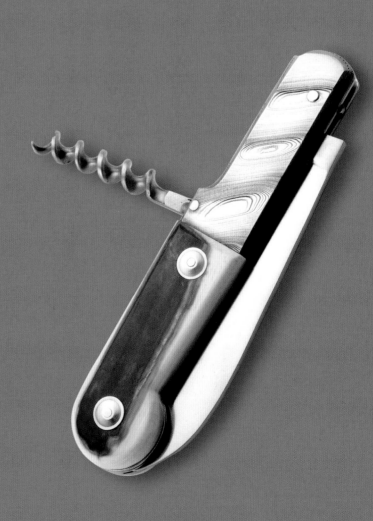

TYPE OF KNIFE
2-part JCH folding knife
(corkscrew and blade)

LOCKING SYSTEM (FOR FOLDING KNIVES)
Slipjoint

STEEL
RWL-34 and bolster
Damascus stainless steel

HANDLE MATERIAL(S)
Mammoth ivory

SIZE
120 mm (closed)

PRICE
★★

ARPAD BOJTOS

As an economist by trade, Arpad Bojtos has been able to travel to many different countries thanks to his primary occupation. It was in the Middle East that he discovered blades that first amazed and then inspired him. It was here that he started his knifemaking journey, as an amateur at first, and then professionally beginning in 1990.

Arpad Bojtos mainly uses manual tools with which he makes sophisticated art knives, which include a lot of chasing and carving. An artist and artisan, Arpad produces few pieces - around ten per year. But you can see why. What a piece! His style, which takes inspiration from the Art Deco movement, is expressed through his favorite themes: animals, nature, mythology and history.

His favorite materials, besides ATS 34 and 440C steel, as well as Damasteel©, are ivory and other fossilized raw materials, mother-of-pearl, gold and silver. Arpad Bojtos is a member of the famous American Knifemaker's Guild. He participates in the most prestigious American knife-making shows, as well as the *Forum International du Couteau Contemporain de Paris* (International Forum of Contemporary Knives, FICX-Paris) at the Carreau du Temple.

www.arpadbojtos.sk

TYPE OF KNIFE
Folding dagger
Clytia and Apollo

LOCKING SYSTEM (FOR FOLDING KNIVES)
Liner lock

STEEL
Damascus stainless steel

HANDLE MATERIAL(S)
Mammoth ivory, gold, silver and mother-of-pearl. Carved inlays representing Clytia and Apollo

SIZE
200 mm (open)

PRICE

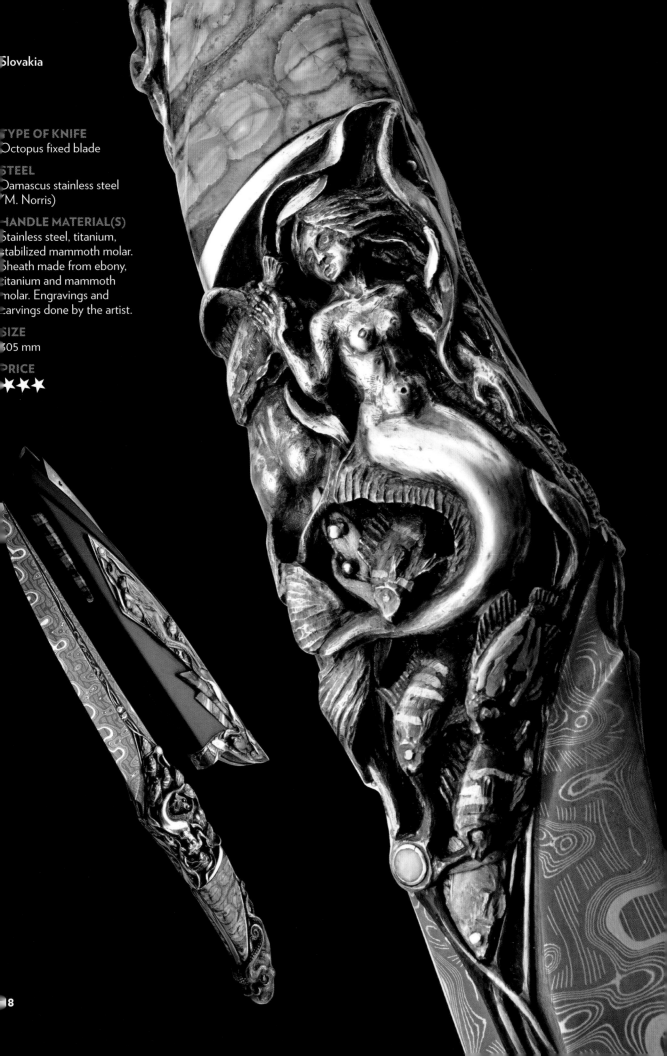

Slovakia

TYPE OF KNIFE
Octopus fixed blade

STEEL
Damascus stainless steel
(M. Norris)

HANDLE MATERIAL(S)
Stainless steel, titanium,
stabilized mammoth molar.
Sheath made from ebony,
titanium and mammoth
molar. Engravings and
carvings done by the artist.

SIZE
305 mm

PRICE
★ ★ ★

TYPE OF KNIFE
Mermaid integral

STEEL
420SS stainless steel

HANDLE MATERIAL(S)
Titanium with gold *inlay*;
stained birch. 3D engraving
done by the artist. Sheath
made from stabilized birch,
ebony, titanium, gold and
silver.

SIZE
280 mm

PRICE
★★★

NICOLAS COUDERC

Nicolas is from Aurillac, in the Auvergne region of France. After having studied plastic and applied arts, he continued his training in Thiers at the CFAI (professional training center)— one of the only two institutions in France to provide a CAP (*certificat d'aptitude professionnelle - certificate of professional competence*) in the relevant field, Cutting Tools and Surgical Instruments. This course was completed in two years and included an internship at a business, on a work-study basis. It was at the Thiers *Musée de la Coutellerie* (Cutlery Museum) that Nicolas was able to apply and refine the skills he learned at the CFAI. On completing his studies, with his CAP in the bag, he had two options. He could go the traditional route, i.e. join one of the many businesses in the city, or he could start his own.

He chose the second option and joined an association of artists and artisans from different backgrounds, "Le Dojo", based in Axat, in the Aude region of France. After searching for his individual style, Nicolas Couderc finally found it. Now it can be recognized anywhere. He goes off the beaten track, his designs are refined, geometric, and would not have disappointed Walter Gropius (Bauhaus). Nicolas is versatile and focuses on modernist, almost iconoclastic, knifemaking design which re-examines traditional ideas. As a knife designer, he makes table knives, folding knives and, notably, elegant multi-blade knives. He likes high-carbon alloy (stainless) steels (D2 and 154 CM) for his blades, and uses modern materials to decorate his handles. If he can't find exactly what wants, he gets creative!

In 2018, Nicolas Couderc received the "*Un des Meilleurs Ouvriers de France*" (French Craftsperson of the Year) award. He participates in the most prestigious French shows, such as Thiers-Coutellia, Nontron in Périgord and FICX-Paris.

www.nicolas-couderc.com

TYPE OF KNIFE
Hemi folding knife

LOCKING SYSTEM (FOR FOLDING KNIVES)
Hidden back lock

STEEL
14C28N

HANDLE MATERIAL(S)
Frame made from Z20 stainless steel with Damascus carbon fiber inserts

SIZE
115 mm (closed)

PRICE
★★

TYPE OF KNIFE
O² folding knife

LOCKING SYSTEM (FOR FOLDING KNIVES)
Slipjoint

STEEL
14C28N

HANDLE MATERIAL(S)
Micro-bead blasted steel and brass

SIZE
90 mm (closed)

PRICE
★★

TYPE OF KNIFE
Folding knife

LOCKING SYSTEM (FOR FOLDING KNIVES)
Slipjoint

STEEL
14C28N

HANDLE MATERIAL(S)
Scales made from computer motherboards

PRICE
★

TYPE OF KNIFE
O² folding knife

LOCKING SYSTEM (FOR FOLDING KNIVES)
Slipjoint

STEEL
14C28N

HANDLE MATERIAL(S)
Stainless steel frame with stabilized colored pencil inserts

SIZE
90 mm (closed)

PRICE
★★

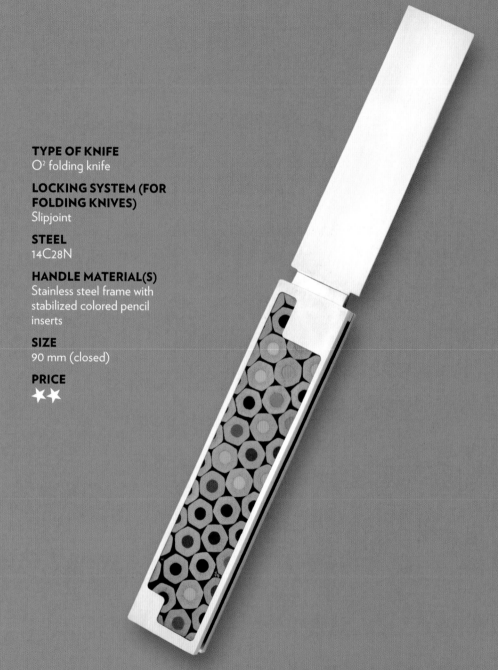

HALEY AND ADAM DESROSIERS

The DesRosiers are a real-life couple, brought together by their shared passion for forging, shooting and the great outdoors. Haley DesRosiers started hammering blades at the age of 17 in a clay forge that she built on her parents' farm in Alaska. Originally from the same region, Adam DesRosiers has lived in close contact with nature for 40 years. In this sometimes hostile environment, knives are an essential tool without which he might not have been able to survive.

Their partnership was, therefore, a no-brainer. Based in Southeast Alaska, Haley and Adam use intricate blacksmithing techniques to craft tools that are as beautiful as they are effective. They primarily make fixed-blade knives, with an integral structure often made from Damascus steel, a technique that they have mastered perfectly. Haley also makes more artistic pieces, such as finely crafted daggers and "Japanese-style" kitchen knives. They place great importance on the sturdiness of their creations, which they have ample opportunity to test in the field...

Both are Mastersmiths in the prestigious American Bladesmith Society and hold Master Classes several times a year. They leave their home in the wilderness to participate in BLADE Show Atlanta and FICX-Paris, but sneak outdoors whenever possible!

www.alaskablades.com

TYPE OF KNIFE
Keyhole integral

STEEL
Composite Damascus

HANDLE MATERIAL(S)
Damascus steel and carbon fiber.
Sheath made from reptile skin by Francesca Ritchie.

PRICE
★★★

OPPOSITE

TYPE OF KNIFE
Semi-integral hunting

STEEL
Twisted multi-bar
Damascus

HANDLE MATERIAL(S)
Sambar deer antlers,
pommel in explosion
Damascus steel

PRICE
★★

TYPE OF KNIFE
Integral Bowie

STEEL
Twisted multi-bar
Damascus

HANDLE MATERIAL(S)
Mammoth ivory

PRICE
★★★

TYPE OF KNIFE
Integral hunting

STEEL
Multi-bar Damascus

HANDLE MATERIAL(S)
Ebony from Mozambique

PRICE
★ ★ ★

France

RAPHAËL DURAND

Born in the Vosges mountain range of France, Raphaël Durand spent his childhood in wide open spaces where the pink of the sandstone mixed with the dark green of the majestic fir trees. Medieval fencing gave him the idea to make his own blades. But fencing blades are large, so, he started with one knife, and then another, then many more!

However, he needed a mentor. He found one in Thiers in Henri Viallon, a respected figure in this little world. Raphaël Durand learned all aspects related to the discipline of forging, including how to make Damascus steel.

Armed with this experience, he decided to become a knifemaker in Villieu, in the Ain region of France. Raphaël Durand is a reserved man and his knives reflect this, without any unnecessary gimmicks, but with an extremely precise finish.

In 2008, he moved to Thiers, in the valley of factories, a unique place along the Durolle river, not far from his mentor, Henri Viallon.

Several years ago, Raphaël went even further and joined the French knife-making elite. He has recently won over American collectors at BLADE Show Atlanta, where he established himself as one of the specialists in the classic folding knife (slipjoint and mid-lock).

His creations respect the practical spirit of knives, but Raphaël transforms them into objects of beauty with sophisticated finishes. His philosophy is purity of form and streamlined mechanisms. The logo that he applies to his blades is a stylized wagon wheel, a symbol of continuous development.

He participates in the major French shows (Coutellia in Thiers and FICX-Paris), as well as BLADE Show Atlanta.

www.raphael-durand.com

TYPE OF KNIFE
Folding knife

LOCKING SYSTEM (FOR FOLDING KNIVES)
Slipjoint

HANDLE MATERIAL(S)
Mammoth ivory with scrimshaw and carving by Serge Raoux

PRICE

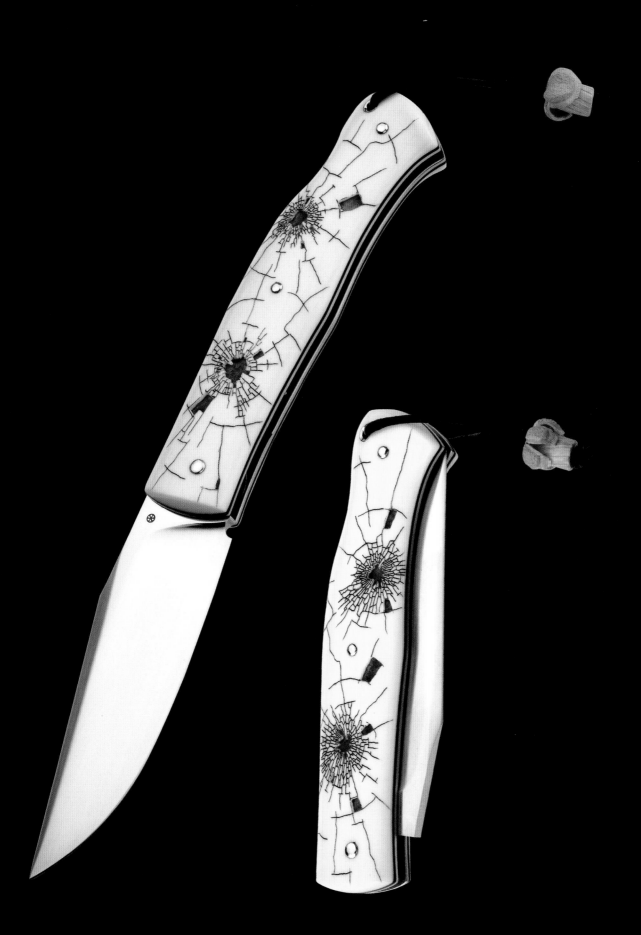

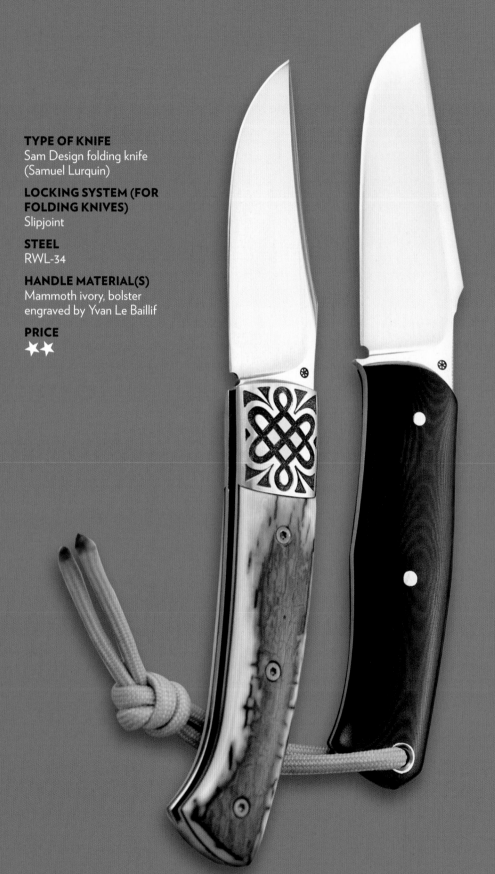

TYPE OF KNIFE
Sam Design folding knife
(Samuel Lurquin)

LOCKING SYSTEM (FOR FOLDING KNIVES)
Slipjoint

STEEL
RWL-34

HANDLE MATERIAL(S)
Mammoth ivory, bolster
engraved by Yvan Le Baillif

PRICE
★★

TYPE OF KNIFE
MPF fixed blade
(*Méchant Petit Fixe*,
Naughty Little Fixed Blade)

STEEL
RWL-34

HANDLE MATERIAL(S)
Black Micarta

PRICE

★

TYPE OF KNIFE
Drop 100 folding knife

LOCKING SYSTEM (FOR FOLDING KNIVES)
Slipjoint

STEEL
RWL-34

HANDLE MATERIAL(S)
Scales made from carved warthog tusk, by Serge Raoux.

PRICE
★★

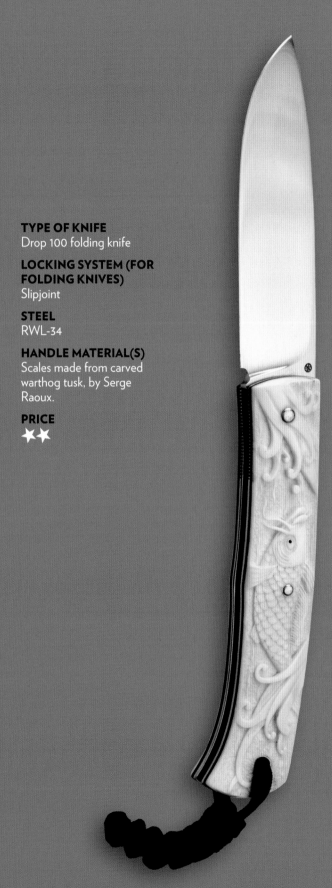

KAY EMBRETSEN

Kay is a knifemaker and blacksmith who has left his mark on the field through his research into Damascus steel. He made a name for himself in 1983 by participating in his first exhibition in his native Sweden, where he already demonstrated a very accomplished collection of typically Nordic hunting knives. He quickly became interested in Damascus steel and his research into new and spectacular patterns lead to the invention of explosion Damascus and the birth of more complex Damascus steels. Kay Embretsen is also involved in the creation of the Damasteel© brand, specializing in the field of powder metallurgy and providing the knifemaking world with a wide range of stainless Damascus patterns.

He is one of the few European knifemakers among the 25 guests invited to the Art Knife Invitational (AKI) in San Diego, which is held every two years and brings together the most prestigious knife artists in the world.

Kay Embretsen's production is focused mainly on luxury folding knives, generally equipped with the classic mid-lock system.

The artist continues to sell his blades to both amateur and professional knifemakers at local events in Sweden. He participates in very few exhibitions outside of his home country: Solvang (California), Las Vegas, AKI and FICX-Paris.

www.embretsenknives.com

TYPE OF KNIFE
Folding knife

LOCKING SYSTEM (FOR FOLDING KNIVES)
Back lock

STEEL
Multi-bar Damascus

HANDLE MATERIAL(S)
Handle made from Damascus steel, engraved insert with gold thread

PRICE
 ★★★

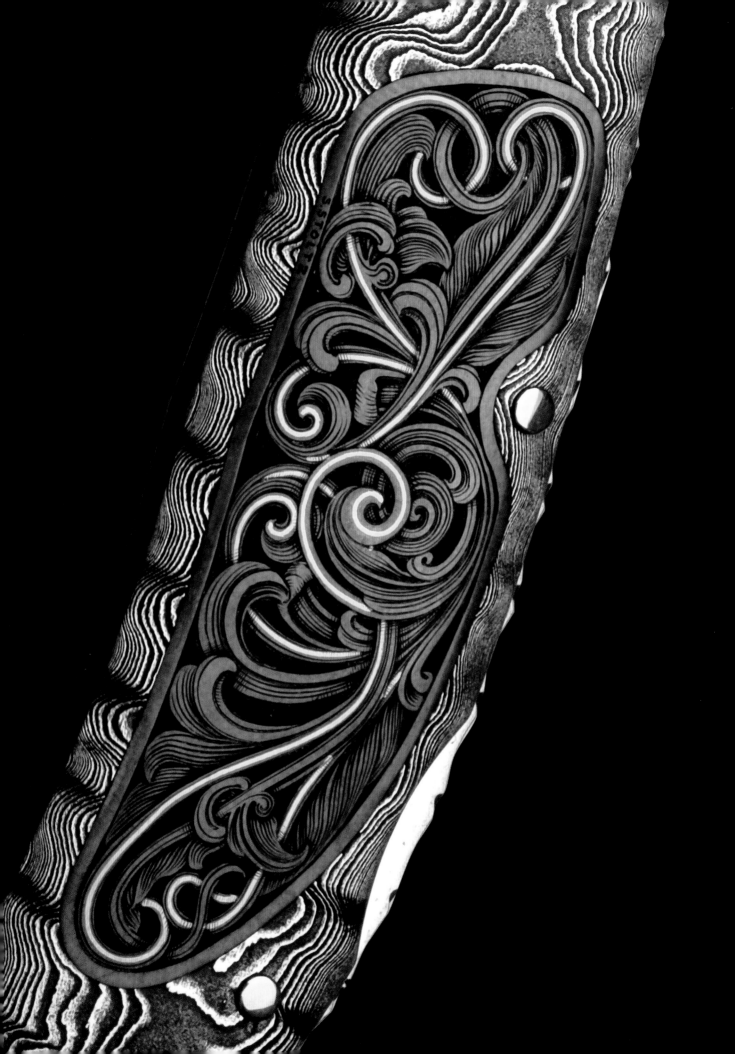

TYPE OF KNIFE
Folding knife

LOCKING SYSTEM (FOR FOLDING KNIVES)
Back lock

STEEL
Damascus steel and bolsters in mosaic Damascus

HANDLE MATERIAL(S)
"Blue" mammoth hide

PRICE
★★★

TYPE OF KNIFE
Folding knife

LOCKING SYSTEM (FOR FOLDING KNIVES)
Back lock

STEEL
Explosion Damascus with Damascus bolsters

HANDLE MATERIAL(S)
"Green" mammoth ivory

PRICE

Sweden

TYPE OF KNIFE
Folding knife

LOCKING SYSTEM (FOR FOLDING KNIVES)
Back lock

STEEL
Explosion Damascus
and Damascus bolsters

HANDLE MATERIAL(S)
Brushed ebony

PRICE
★★★

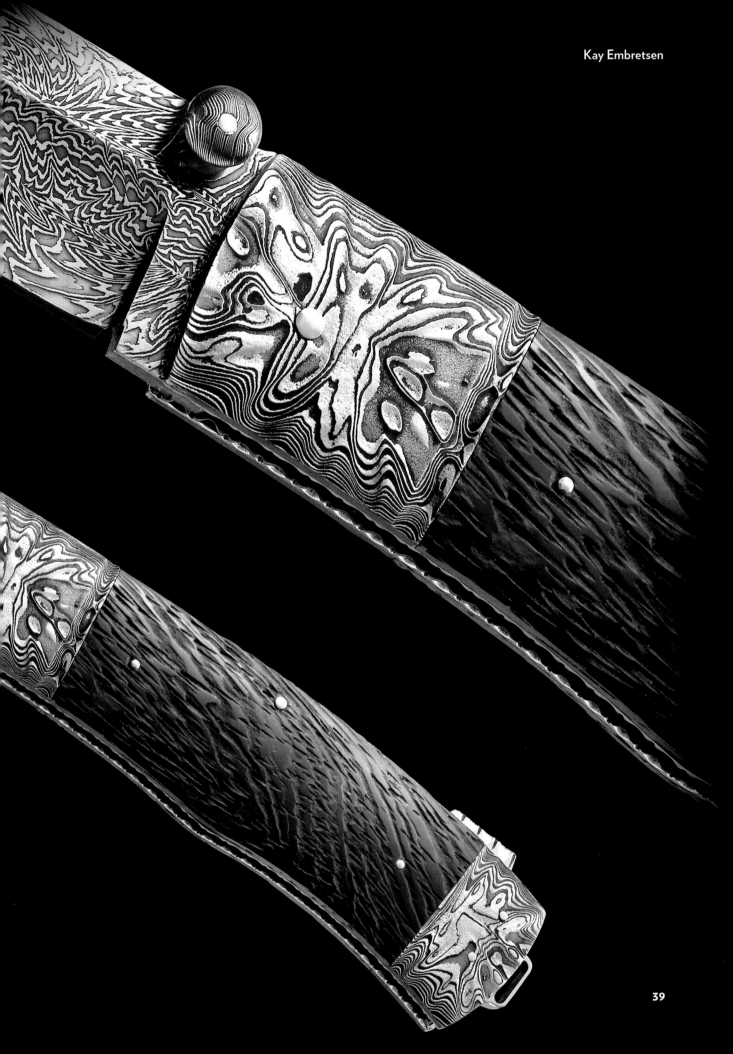

EMMANUEL ESPOSITO

Emmanuel Esposito was born in 1983 in the province of Turin, in the Piedmont region of Italy. Ever since he was little, he has loved showing his imagination in different ways. His profound interest in engineering, inherited from his grandfather, and his passion for nature and hunting inevitably drew him to gunsmithing and knifemaking. It was through reading that he learnt about knifemaking culture: he studied the big names in the field at the time, their techniques, the materials they used, etc. He left nothing to chance, meticulously scrutinizing each detail and absorbing all the information (Emmanuel was a fanatic).

When he made his first knives at the age of 18, specialists sensed the emergence of a truly innovative style. At twenty, he joined the Italian Knifemakers Guild (CIC) and was awarded the coveted title of "Maestro". He is considered a gifted knifemaker by his peers and collectors know this, purchasing knives as soon as they are put up for sale at the Milan show (and even beforehand). He excels in all categories: integral fixed blade knives, folding knives with sophisticated mechanisms, material inserts (interframe), and even clock movement mechanisms! His knives bring the ancient and modern together, sometimes with retro-futuristic elements (a reference to *steampunk*). His knives are few and far between, and the prices go *up, up, up*!

His favorite materials are mother of pearl, which he uses in mosaics and adds to his handles, usually made from 416 stainless steel. He also uses modern synthetic materials, such as different colored carbon fibers, Bakelite, micarta, etc., which he pairs with gold, bronze, mokume-gane or even Damascus stainless steel. For his blades, he likes to use RWL-34 steel and Damascus. Emmanuel Esposito participates in the most prestigious shows: Milan, San Diego, Solvang (California).

www.emmanuelmaker.it

TYPE OF KNIFE
Dolphin folding knife

LOCKING SYSTEM (FOR FOLDING KNIVES)
Inspired by clock parts

STEEL
RWL-34

HANDLE MATERIAL(S)
416 stainless steel frame with mother-of-pearl mosaic inserts

SIZE
190 mm (open)

PRICE
★★★★

TYPE OF KNIFE
Folding dagger

James Bond Dagger

**LOCKING SYSTEM
(FOR FOLDING
KNIVES)**
C-Lock 01

STEEL
RWL-34

HANDLE MATERIAL(S)
Frame made from 416
stainless steel, insert made
from mokume, and mosaic
made from mother-of-
pearl and black bakelite

SIZE
200 mm (open)

PRICE

OPPOSITE

TYPE OF KNIFE
Rhyno integral (2007)

STEEL
RWL-34

HANDLE MATERIAL(S)
Green canvas micarta
scales

SIZE
205 mm

PRICE
Prototype

Italy

TYPE OF KNIFE
Cherokee folding knife

LOCKING SYSTEM (FOR FOLDING KNIVES)
Piston lock

STEEL
RWL-34

HANDLE MATERIAL(S)
Timascus scales

SIZE
210 mm (open)

PRICE

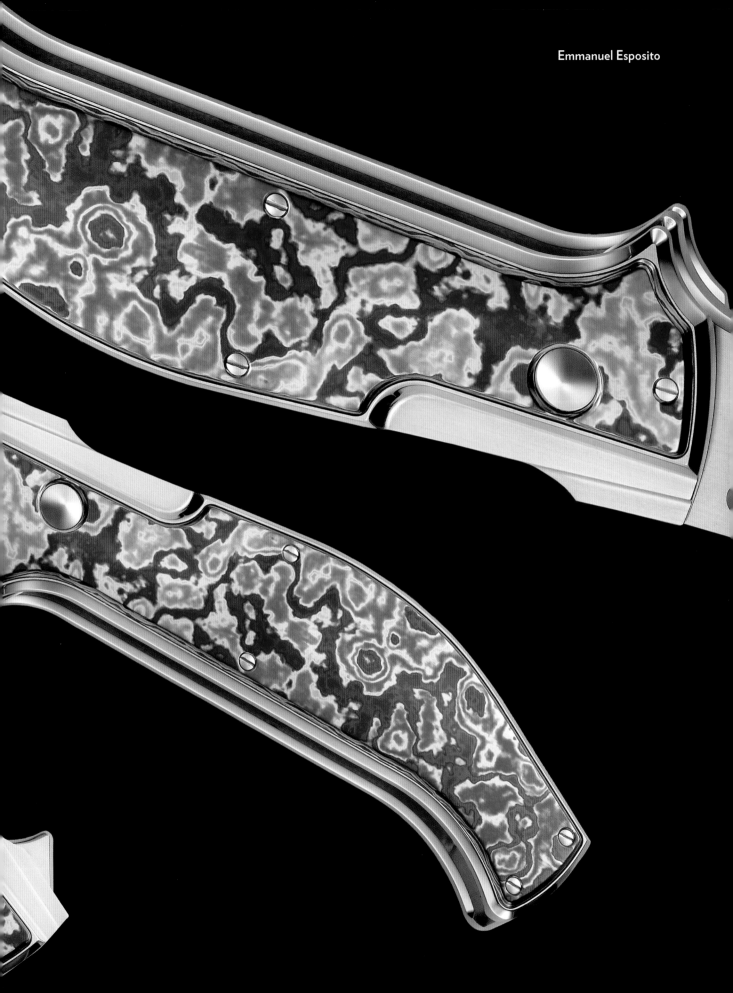

ANTONIO FOGARIZZU

Be careful, or you might mistake one Fogarizzu for another! Coming from a long line of Sardinian knifemakers, Antonio was born (and lives) in the knife-making city of Pattada. Within the Italian guild, there are four Fogarizzus. His father is Salvatore "Tore" Fogarizzu.

He inherited Sardinian knifemaking traditions from his family, and it still shines through in some of his folding knives in the very assertive Pattadese style. But he has generally broken away from this to give us explosive, exuber-ant, overflowing knifemaking, combining the baroque with the modern, the classic with the revolutionary.

He trusts the best engravers to decorate some of his pieces, sometimes to a great extent. These have included Pedretti, Torcoli, Pedersoli and Peli, to name a few. Antonio Fogarizzu likes to work with precious materials: various mother-of-pearls, antique tortoiseshell, fossilized mammoth ivory, inlaid gold, etc... but also with the most modern materials for his futuristic creations, including carbon fiber, Bakelite, and beryllium bronze. He uses a lot of heat-colored mosaic Damascus, which he makes himself. The price of some of his knives, richly engraved, can be sky high.

He participates in the most prestigious exhibitions, in Europe and the United States.

TYPE OF KNIFE
Folding dagger
Calamo Dagger

LOCKING SYSTEM (FOR FOLDING KNIVES)
Push-button

STEEL
M390

HANDLE MATERIAL(S)
Frame made from B419 steel with carbon fiber and mother-of-pearl inserts

SIZE
225 mm (open)

PRICE

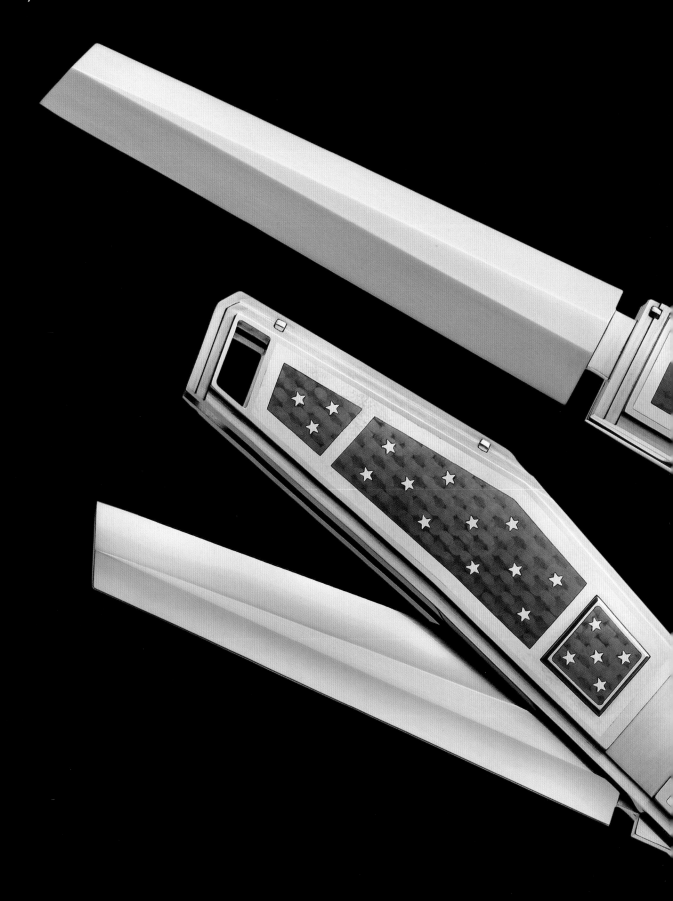

TYPE OF KNIFE
Cube Box Opener folding knife

LOCKING SYSTEM (FOR FOLDING KNIVES)
Push-button

STEEL
RWL-34

HANDLE MATERIAL(S)
Body made of 416 stainless steel, carbon fiber inserts. Screws, bolts and decoration in gold.

PRICE
★★★★

Italy

TYPE OF KNIFE
Folding dagger

**LOCKING SYSTEM (FOR
FOLDING KNIVES)**
Mid-lock

STEEL
RWL-34

HANDLE MATERIAL(S)
Frame in 416 stainless steel.
Inserts in black mother-of-
pearl and gold. Engravings
by Manrico Torcoli.

SIZE
210 mm (open)

PRICE
★★★★

TYPE OF KNIFE
Cube Evo folding knife

LOCKING SYSTEM (FOR FOLDING KNIVES)
Push-button

STEEL
RWL-34

HANDLE MATERIAL(S)
Frame made from 416 steel
with carbon fiber and gold
inserts

SIZE
200 mm (open)

PRICE

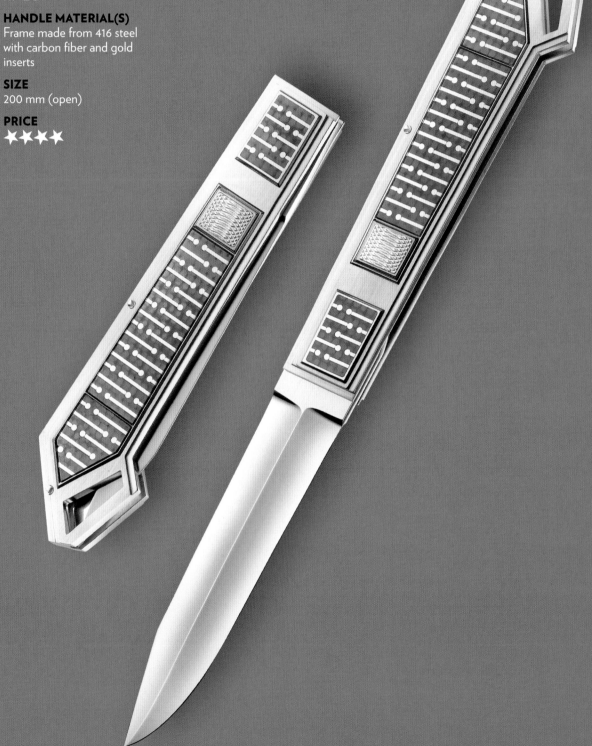

MARCELLO GARAU

With a career in agronomics, this islander was only familiar with the traditional knifemaking culture of his native Sardinia. His first knives, made as a self-taught artist, were inspired by this. When he first started out, he had very little contact with the knifemaking world. It was through reading specialist magazines and books that he discovered this world and he perfected his technique.

Today, Marcello Garau is internationally recognized as one of the masters of modern Italian knifemaking, and his pieces (mainly folding knives with complex locking systems) are sought by collectors from all over the world. He particularly likes precious material inserts (stones and mother-of-pearls) in the highly polished steel of his stainless steel handles. Reserved and thoughtful, he is the master of all production stages of his creations. The Sardinian influence can be seen in his work, even in his more recent pieces.

He participates in the Milan show, FICX-Paris and a few big shows across the Atlantic.

www.knifecreator.com

TYPE OF KNIFE
Mondrianesque folding knife

LOCKING SYSTEM (FOR FOLDING KNIVES)
Push button, in the handle

STEEL
RWL-34

HANDLE MATERIAL(S)
416 stainless steel frame with coral, mother-of-pearl, lapis lazuli and Damascus inserts

SIZE
220 mm (open)

PRICE

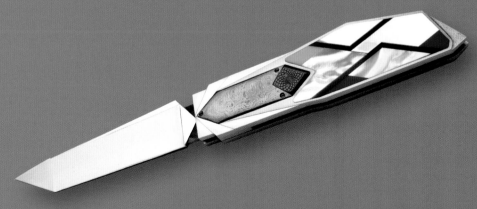

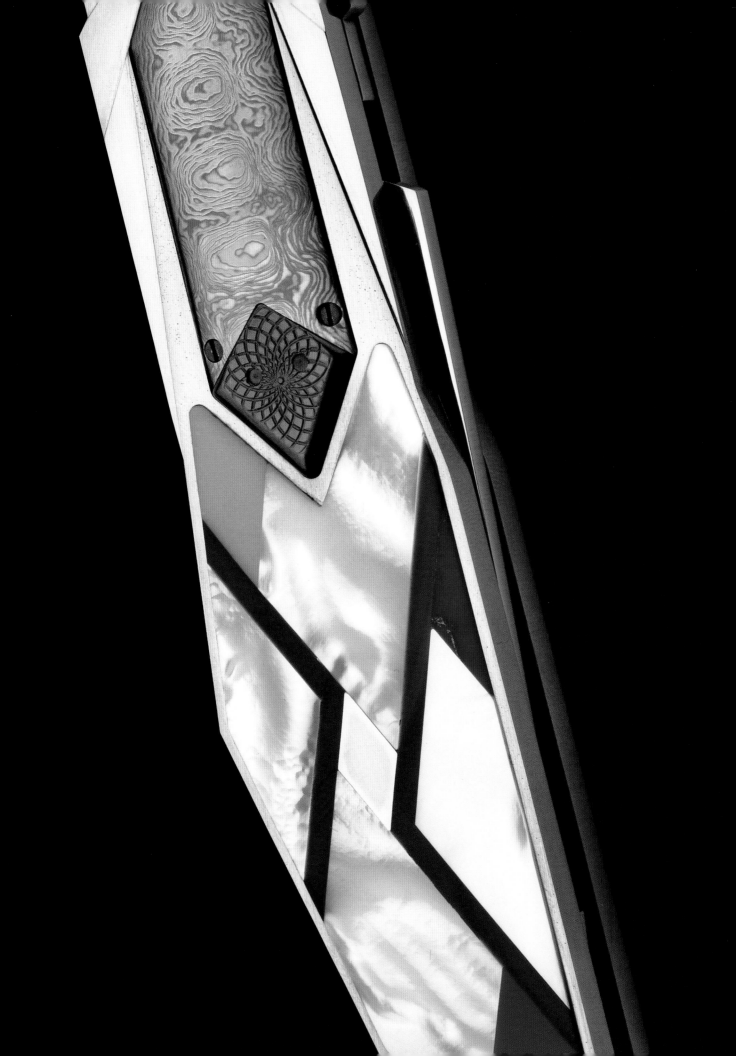

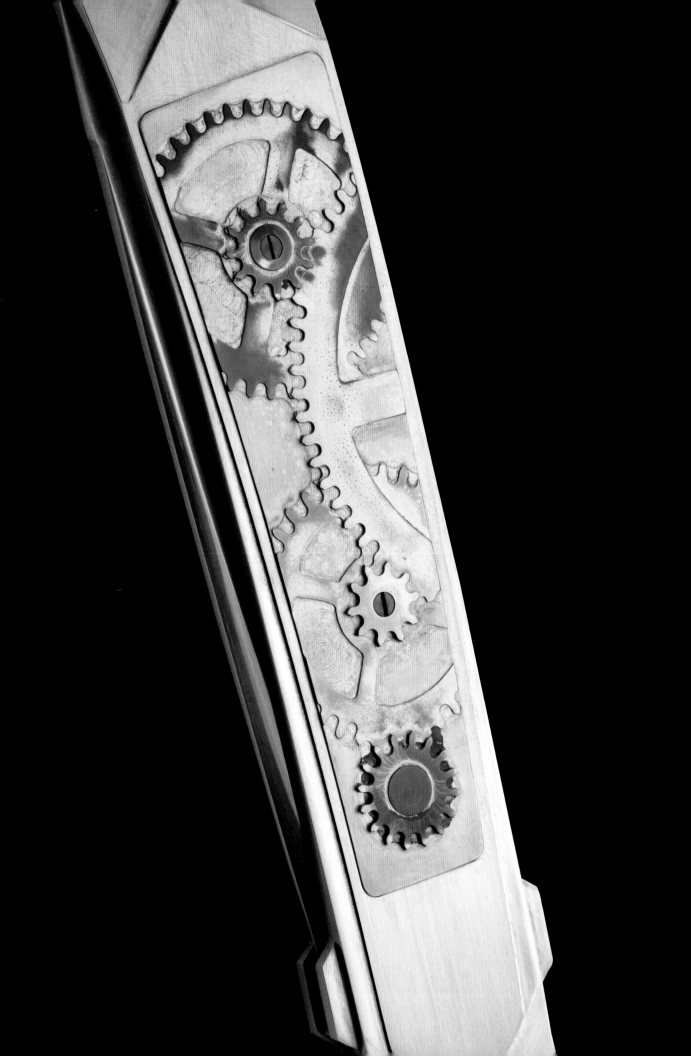

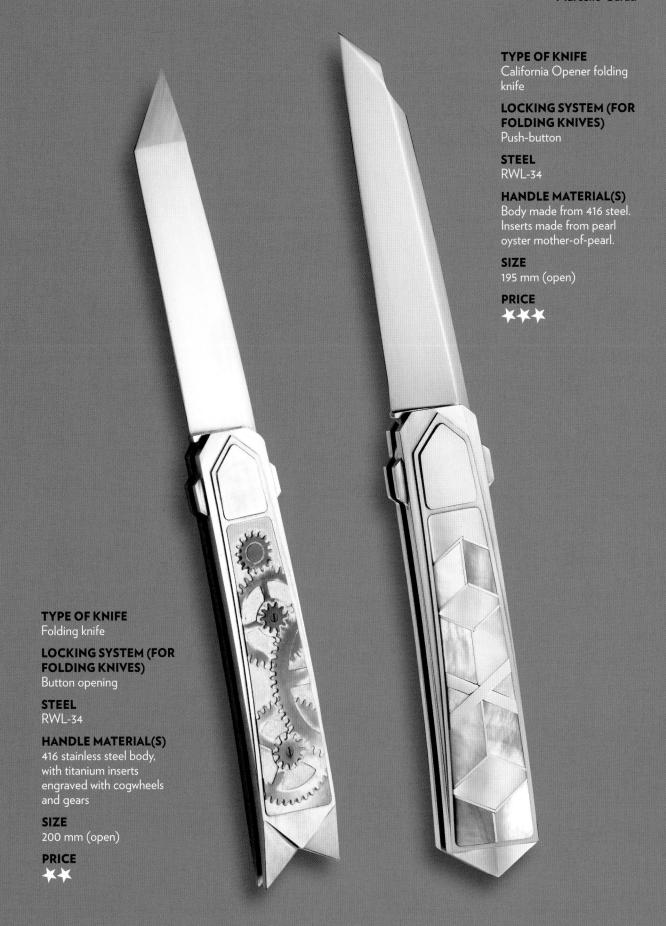

TYPE OF KNIFE
California Opener folding
knife

**LOCKING SYSTEM (FOR
FOLDING KNIVES)**
Push-button

STEEL
RWL-34

HANDLE MATERIAL(S)
Body made from 416 steel.
Inserts made from pearl
oyster mother-of-pearl.

SIZE
195 mm (open)

PRICE
★★★

TYPE OF KNIFE
Folding knife

**LOCKING SYSTEM (FOR
FOLDING KNIVES)**
Button opening

STEEL
RWL-34

HANDLE MATERIAL(S)
416 stainless steel body,
with titanium inserts
engraved with cogwheels
and gears

SIZE
200 mm (open)

PRICE
★★

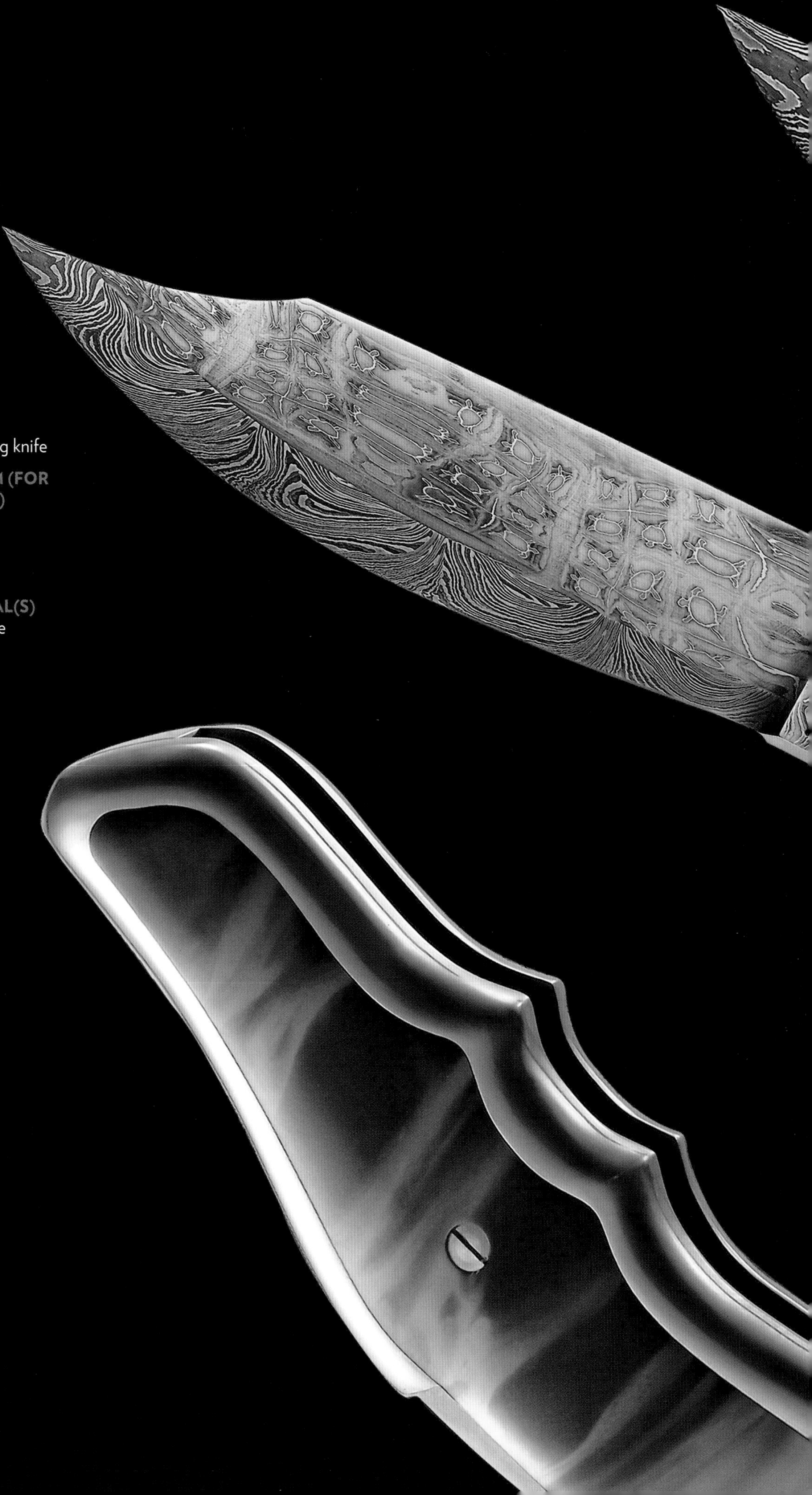

Italy

TYPE OF KNIFE
Foggia Antica folding knife

LOCKING SYSTEM (FOR FOLDING KNIVES)
Back lock

STEEL
Mosaic Damascus

HANDLE MATERIAL(S)
416 steel with antique tortoiseshell inserts

SIZE
198 mm (open)

PRICE
★★

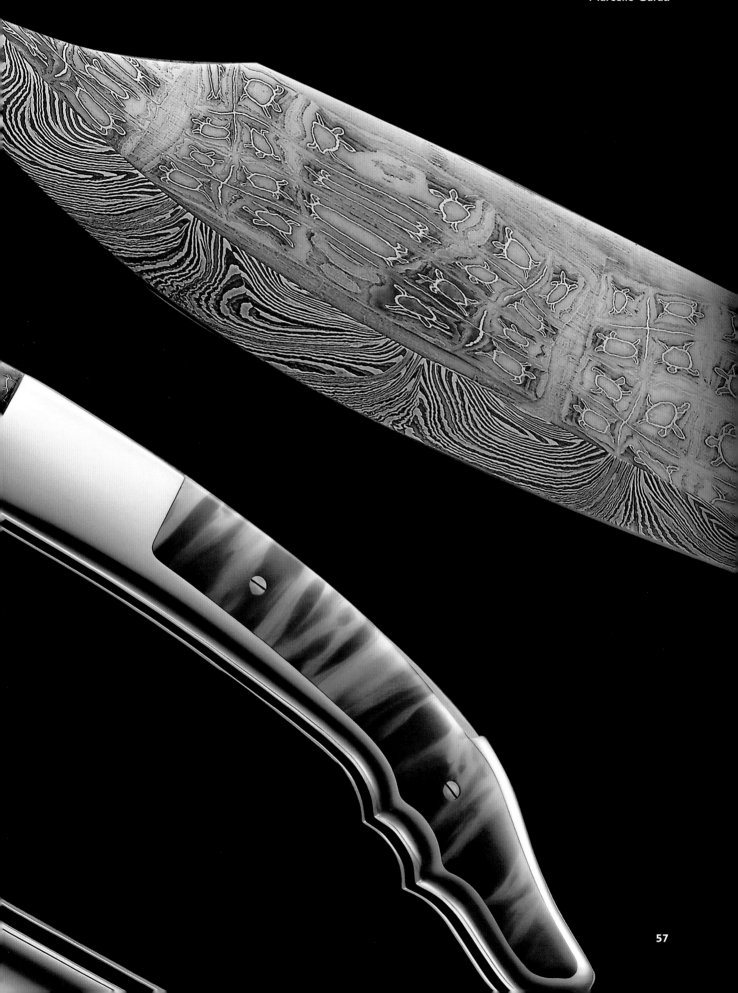

ALAIN GRANGETTE

Alain Grangette is completely self-taught. As an amateur, he built his forge in 1998. At the time, he had a very academic approach towards knifemaking. Through work, trial and error, his first knives were made in 2000. He participated in his first exhibition in Thiers, the French capital of knifemaking, not far from his home in Creuse.

Today, Alain Grangette has a new workshop equipped with modern machines, but his old forge is still there. He is passionate about clockmaking, armory and goldsmithing, from which he draws a lot of inspiration. His folding knives, which all have complex mechanisms, are unique pieces with often futuristic designs.

He participates in prestigious shows, but doesn't forget those of his hometown of Creuse, more modest but so much fun! Masgot (23), Guéret, FICX - Paris, Miami, New York.

www.alaingrangette.com

TYPE OF KNIFE
Folding dagger

LOCKING SYSTEM (FOR FOLDING KNIVES)
Sliding blade

STEEL
RWL-34

HANDLE MATERIAL(S)
Mother-of-pearl insert

PRICE
★★

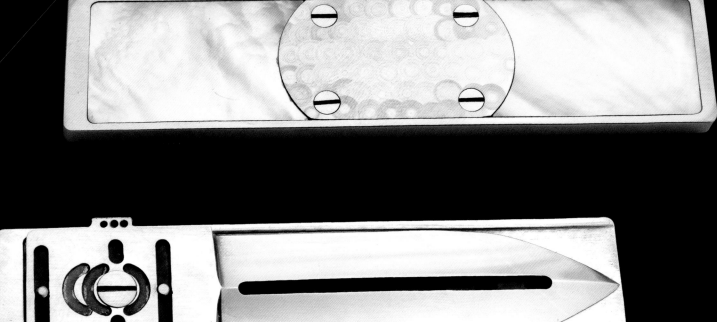

TYPE OF KNIFE
Creuse folding knife

LOCKING SYSTEM (FOR FOLDING KNIVES)
Ratchet lock (anti-return device)

STEEL
RWL-34

HANDLE MATERIAL(S)
416 stainless steel with stabilized mammoth molar inserts

PRICE
★★

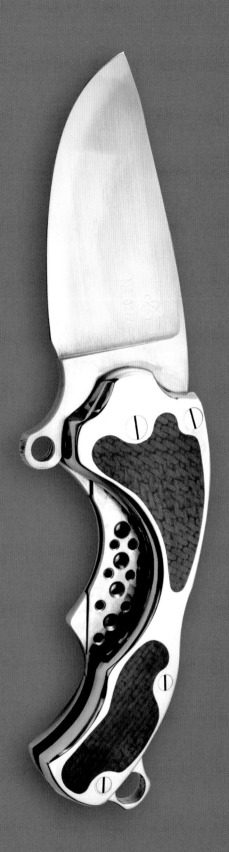

TYPE OF KNIFE
Tactical folding knife

LOCKING SYSTEM (FOR FOLDING KNIVES)
Improved liner lock

STEEL
N690

HANDLE MATERIAL(S)
416 steel with carbon fiber inserts

PRICE
★★

KOJI AND DEW HARA

Koji Hara, despite his youthful appearance, is over sixty! Born in 1949, he was one of the knifemakers who revolutionized Japanese knifemaking, which had been locked into tradition until the early 1980s.

Koji made his first knife in 1988 and showed his first collection in 1991 at the Seki exhibition, the biggest knifemaking city in Japan. There was not much opportunity for *custom* knifemaking in Japan, so it was in the United States that Koji found success: he joined the very prominent American Knifemaker's Guild in 1994. Since then, he has not stopped travelling around the United States, Europe and Asia (Japan and Taiwan). He is probably the most well-travelled knifemaker in the world!

Koji designs and makes knives in a very personal, instantly recognizable style. Whether they are fixed blades, minimalist folding knives (traditional Japanese higonokami) or flipper knives, Japanese culture can be seen in all his pieces. He particularly likes using pearl oyster and abalone mother-of-pearl in his handles. As for the blades, he mainly uses Cowry-Y steel, which is made using the powder metallurgy process (Daido Steel), which gives an impeccable polished mirror effect.

Dew Hara is Koji's son. He learned about knifemaking from his father, but has developed his own distinctly modern style. He mainly produces high-end tactical knives, and also works with the American manufacturer Columbia River Knives and Tools (CRKT). He has a long career ahead of him.

www.knifehousehara.com

TYPE OF KNIFE
Higo Naïfu folding knife
(Koji Hara)

**LOCKING SYSTEM (FOR
FOLDING KNIVES)**
Friction (no blade locking)

STEEL
VGold 10 suminagashi san
mai

HANDLE MATERIAL(S)
Carved "take" and
burnished copper handle

SIZE
190 mm (open)

PRICE

Japan

TYPE OF KNIFE
Maki-e folding knife - Four
seasons (Koji Hara)

**LOCKING SYSTEM (FOR
FOLDING KNIVES)**
Liner lock

STEEL
Cowry X

HANDLE MATERIAL(S)
316 steel.
Maki-e lacquer on mother-
of-pearl

PRICE
★★★★

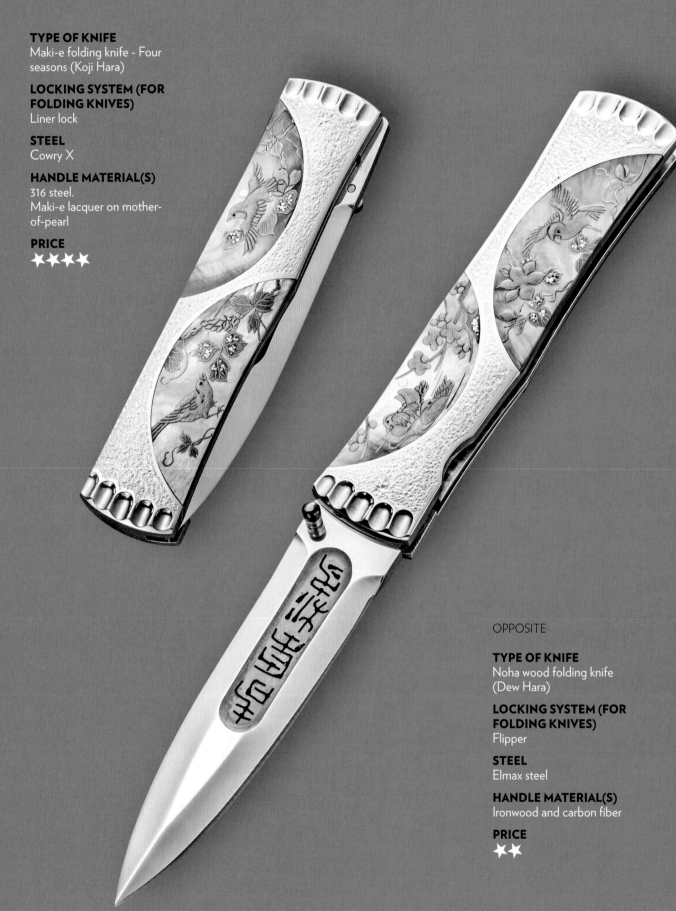

OPPOSITE

TYPE OF KNIFE
Noha wood folding knife
(Dew Hara)

**LOCKING SYSTEM (FOR
FOLDING KNIVES)**
Flipper

STEEL
Elmax steel

HANDLE MATERIAL(S)
Ironwood and carbon fiber

PRICE
★★

MATHIEU HERRERO

Mathieu Herrero (born in 1977) began his career making string instruments, in England, then Aurillac, where he moved in 2004. It was difficult to make a living from string instruments, especially in the provinces: the trade was becoming more and more industrialized, with a lot of instruments being made in Asia. The work of a specialized artisan was often more expensive than the instrument itself.

Deeply disappointed by this as he loved his trade, in 2010, Mathieu considered retraining and taking advantage of his know-how in another specialized trade. Why not knifemaking?

His older brother had been collecting fine art knives for a long time and showed Mathieu a few made by well-known knifemakers. He advised Mathieu to try it out, recommending that he take focus on folding knives.

The idea caught on. Mathieu studied the beautiful folding knives from his brother's collection in detail, including pieces by Raphaël Durand, Nicolas Couderc, Laurent Gaillard and even Mickaël Moing. Then he discovered Robert Beillonnet's work.

While he loved antique string instrument techniques (especially viola d'amores), he developed a similar love for knifemaking from times gone by: simple pieces from the late medieval era — everyday knives from the late 14th and early 15th centuries, such as those featured in the English book *Knives and Scabbards*; the knifemaking of Langres and Nogent, and of Châtellerault; the elegant fruit knives and other gentlemen's knives from the 18th century, not to mention the regional knives that have worn down the pockets of our farmers for decades:

Charlois, Jambette, Rouennais, Laguiole, Aurillac, Saint-Martin, and knives from the great Sheffield era. Today, he is considered one of the most gifted knifemakers by his peers.

Mathieu Herrero participates in most French shows and in 2019, he attended the huge BLADE Show Atlanta.

TYPE OF KNIFE
Mother-of-pearl folding knife

LOCKING SYSTEM (FOR FOLDING KNIVES)
Slipjoint

STEEL
XC-75

HANDLE MATERIAL(S)
Inspired by 18th-century knives; black mother-of-pearl and nickel silver

SIZE
120 mm (closed)

PRICE

France

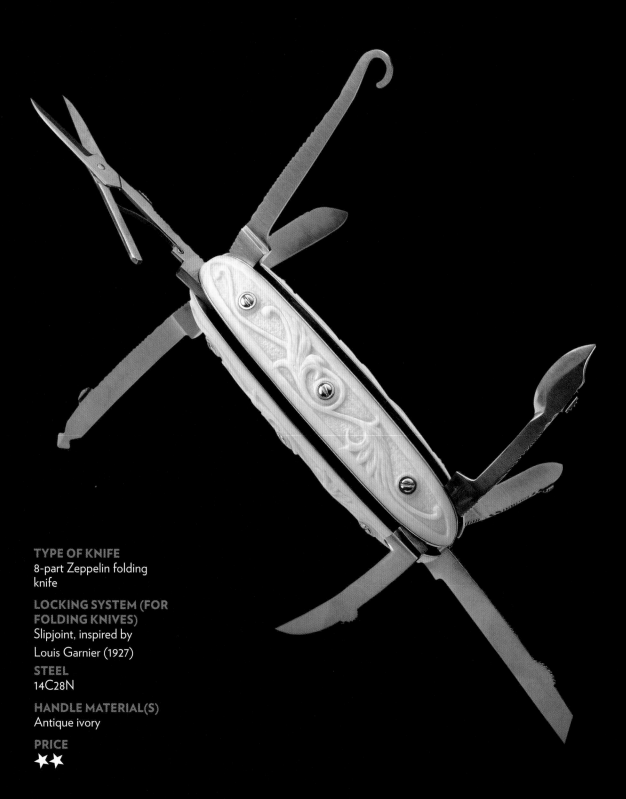

TYPE OF KNIFE
8-part Zeppelin folding
knife

**LOCKING SYSTEM (FOR
FOLDING KNIVES)**
Slipjoint, inspired by

Louis Garnier (1927)

STEEL
14C28N

HANDLE MATERIAL(S)
Antique ivory

PRICE
★★

TYPE OF KNIFE
11-part folding Fisherman's Knife, inspired by Sheffield knifemaking

LOCKING SYSTEM (FOR FOLDING KNIVES)
Slipjoint

STEEL
14C28N

HANDLE MATERIAL(S)
Brass plates, nickel silver shield and marbled carbon fiber scales

PRICE
★★

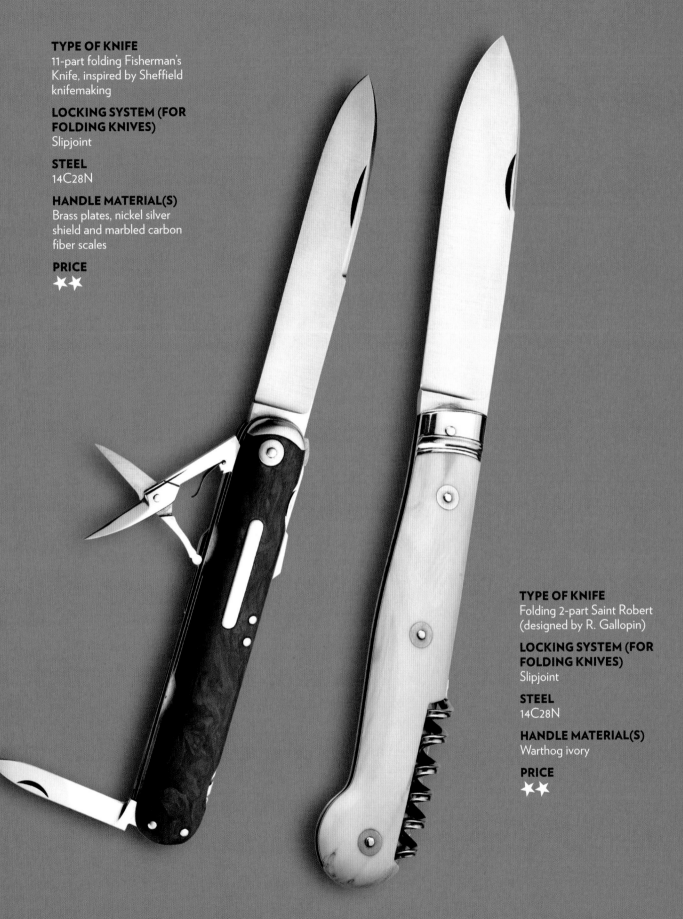

TYPE OF KNIFE
Folding 2-part Saint Robert (designed by R. Gallopin)

LOCKING SYSTEM (FOR FOLDING KNIVES)
Slipjoint

STEEL
14C28N

HANDLE MATERIAL(S)
Warthog ivory

PRICE
★★

HARUMI HIRAYAMA

Harumi Hirayama was born in Tokyo in 1960. It was at the Tama Art University that she became interested in knifemaking, choosing kitchen knives as the theme of her final design project. After leaving university, Harumi worked for some time at the design office of a company that manufactures consumer goods. But this work did not fulfill her artistic dreams, and in 1985 she threw herself into the world of fine art knives, attempting to create modern designs while using classic Japanese craft techniques and materials for their decoration. This was an innovative approach, if ever there was one, at a time when the majority of new artisan knifemakers limited themselves to slavishly imitating the models produced by the American Bob Loveless! Success quickly followed.

She makes few knives (between 10 and 25 per year) and her delivery times vary between three to six years, depending on the complexity of the knife being commissioned and after a long written exchange with her customer. Harumi's knives are based on several themes: the seasons, the atmosphere, insects (dragonflies and butterflies), flowers (cherry blossoms in particular; the *sakura* is the national flower of Japan), water and the sea, owls and... cats. She works almost exclusively without machines, using only a small band saw and a mini drill. She does everything else with a file, and then any marks are removed with a stone after heat treatment. She does her decorative work with goldsmiths' and jewelers' tools, with the same attention to detail.

Harumi Hirayama attends few knife shows: the one organized by the American Guild, of which she is a member (usually every three years), the small Matsumoto show and the Knife and Life Show in Taipei. She has previously participated in the FICX - Paris exhibition.

www.ne.jp/asahi/harumi/knives

TYPE OF KNIFE
Pair of Pico folding knives with dragonflies and butterflies

LOCKING SYSTEM (FOR FOLDING KNIVES)
Mid-lock

STEEL
440C

HANDLE MATERIAL(S)
Ironwood with inlaid mother-of-pearl and semi-precious stone patterns

PRICE

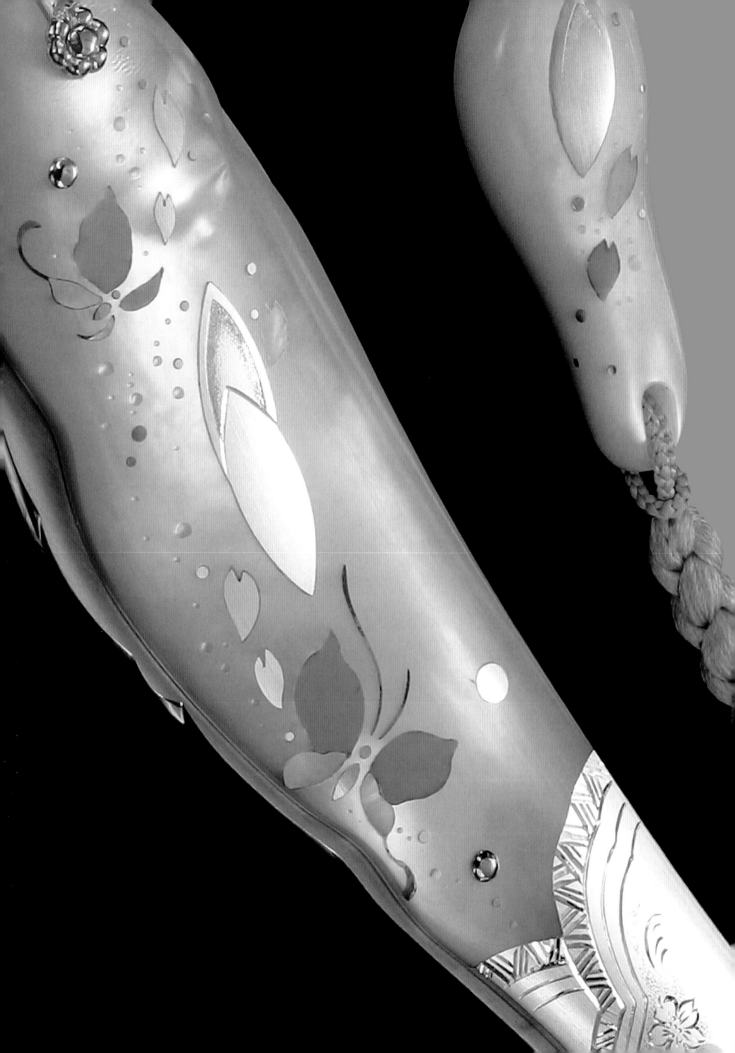

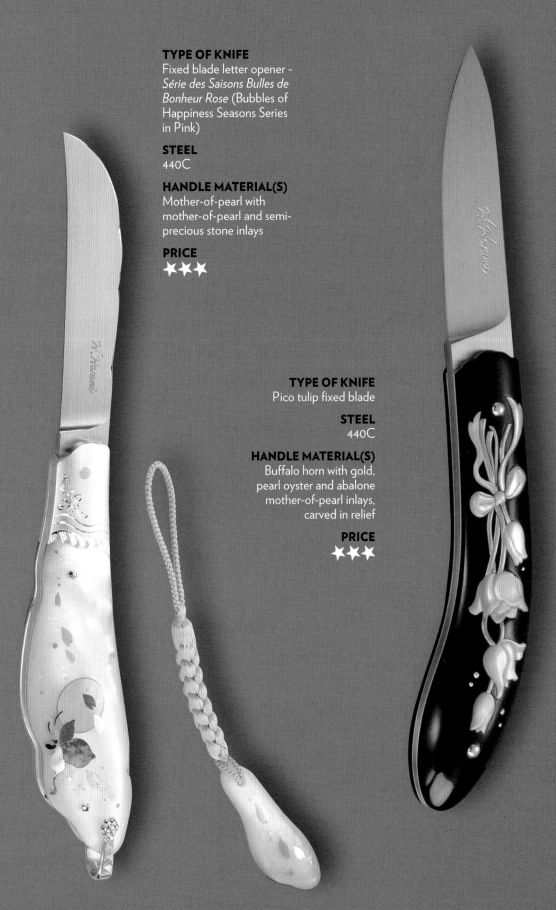

TYPE OF KNIFE
Fixed blade letter opener -
*Série des Saisons Bulles de
Bonheur Rose* (Bubbles of
Happiness Seasons Series
in Pink)

STEEL
440C

HANDLE MATERIAL(S)
Mother-of-pearl with
mother-of-pearl and semi-
precious stone inlays

PRICE
★★★

TYPE OF KNIFE
Pico tulip fixed blade

STEEL
440C

HANDLE MATERIAL(S)
Buffalo horn with gold,
pearl oyster and abalone
mother-of-pearl inlays,
carved in relief

PRICE
★★★

DES
HORN

Des Horn started making knives during his childhood. He abandoned knife-making while completing his dental surgery studies, before quickly coming back to it in a more serious way. He took part in high-level competitive shooting at the same time.

A scientist by training, it is with the same level of dedication that he started his career as a knifemaker 30 years ago. He leaves nothing to chance with his knives and performs the heat treatment on his blades himself, after carefully choosing the steels. He uses RWL-34 steel and Damasteel© stainless Damascus steel, both made using the powder metallurgy process, and a cryogenic treatment which helps him to achieve an exceptional level of hardness (61 to 63 on the Rockwell scale). For the handles, he uses Damasteel ©, meteorite, mammoth ivory, mother-of-pearl and a South African wood known as *pink ivory* (a vibrant pink color).

He exhibits his work in Thiers (Coutellia) as well as at the two Paris shows (FICX and SICAC) and in Milan.

www.deshorn.com

TYPE OF KNIFE
Flipper folding knife

LOCKING SYSTEM (FOR FOLDING KNIVES)
Liner lock

STEEL
Damasteel©

HANDLE MATERIAL(S)
Damasteel© and zirconium bolster, lightning strike carbon fiber scales

PRICE
★★

TYPE OF KNIFE
Galaxy folding dagger

LOCKING SYSTEM (FOR FOLDING KNIVES)
Mid-lock

STEEL
Damascus stainless steel

HANDLE MATERIAL(S)
M315 steel engraved by Julien Marchal, inspired by the "*Petit Prince*" (The Little Prince) by Saint Exupéry

PRICE

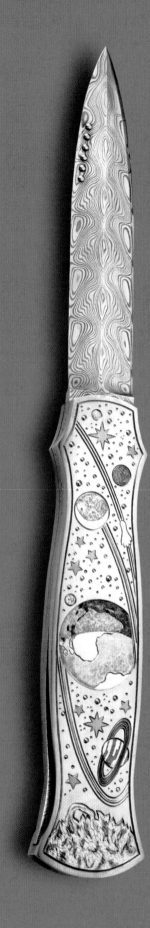

TYPE OF KNIFE
Folding knife

LOCKING SYSTEM (FOR FOLDING KNIVES)
Ball plunger locking

STEEL
Damasteel©

HANDLE MATERIAL(S)
Sides made from pietersite (Namibian semi-precious stone), miter engraved by Julien Marchal

PRICE
★★

JACQUES JOBIN

Jacques Jobin made his first knife in 1985, for fun, and was quickly caught up in this passion. The eldest of a family of nine children, he was born in 1951 and has always lived in Lévis, on the banks of the St. Lawrence River, just across from Quebec. His youth was influenced by early space and deep sea exploration. Primarily thanks to Captain Cousteau and his films and books, Jacques began to take an interest in scuba diving in 1965, using the first commercially available model of twin-hose regulator that he had helped design.

He received his pilot's license in 1975 and was passionate about anything that flew. In 1975, he became a bodyguard after a training period at the Nicolet Police Institute. From 1985 to 1990, he was a part-time knifemaker before taking the plunge in 1991. Since then, he has participated in several international knifemaking shows, such as the BLADE Show in the United States and his favorite, SICAC, in Paris.

Jacques Jobin mainly uses ATS-34 steel for his blades, as well as Damascus steel made by Darryl Meier, Devin Thomas and Damasteel©. He works with a very wide range of materials, including titanium, which he uses extensively for the handles of his folding knives and futuristic pieces (pronounced "tsitsane" in Québecois French). He makes some futuristic and carved pieces, and few truly classic knives: even his Laguiole knives have a little something avant-garde about them. His folding knives use their own ambidextrous, one-handed locking system, as demonstrated on his "Chrysalis" model. Jacques Jobin works without a template, so all of his models are unique.

Today, he is semi-retired and sells his goods via his website.

www.jjobin.com

TYPE OF KNIFE
Folding knife with locking system

LOCKING SYSTEM (FOR FOLDING KNIVES)
Top-operated lock

STEEL
Damascus stainless steel

HANDLE MATERIAL(S)
Titanium plates, mammoth ivory

SIZE
127 mm (closed)

PRICE
★★

TYPE OF KNIFE
Futuristic dagger

STEEL
ATS-34

HANDLE MATERIAL(S)
"Cockpit" handle in
anodized titanium, topped
with mother-of-pearl

SIZE
480 mm

PRICE
★★★★

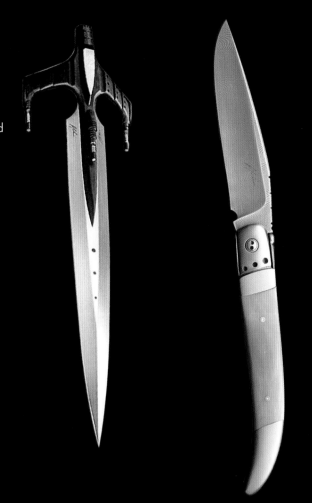

TYPE OF KNIFE
Interpretation of a
Laguiole-style folding knife

**LOCKING SYSTEM (FOR
FOLDING KNIVES)**
Slipjoint

STEEL
Damascus steel by Devin
Thomas

HANDLE MATERIAL(S)
Anodized titanium and
mammoth ivory plates

SIZE
127 mm (closed)

PRICE
★★

TYPE OF KNIFE
Folding knife with locking
system

**LOCKING SYSTEM (FOR
FOLDING KNIVES)**
Top-operated lock

STEEL
Stainless Damascus steel
by Devin Thomas

HANDLE MATERIAL(S)
Anodized titanium
and pearl oyster mother-
of-pearl

SIZE
127 mm (closed)

PRICE
★★

PHILIPPE JOURGET

Philippe Jourget trained in woodworking before obtaining a qualification in artistic trades, specifically armory (in Saint-Etienne). He lives in Puy-en-Velay (Haute-Loire). His history with knifemaking goes back to his childhood, when he dreamed that one day he would make a living in the trade. He set aside the idea before returning to it, completely obsessed! He even went so far as to take a forging course with Jean-Jacques Astier. These days he is a full-time knifemaker.

Philippe is particularly interested in the engineering aspect of knives; you don't mess about with precision when you've been trained in armory! He believes: "If it's beautiful, that's a plus... but first it has to fit together perfectly!" Let's just say the hundredth of a millimeter is his favorite unit of measurement. He works in close collaboration with French designer Tashi Bharucha.

His creations are varied and he tries to sell his knives at affordable prices, even though his collection is increasingly made up of very technically accomplished folding knives: liner lock or frame lock with flipper, made from high-tech materials (CPM-154 or RWL-34 steel, carbon fiber, anodized titanium, etc.).

He participates in the FICX-Paris exhibition, as well as the Atlanta BLADE Show.

www.philippejourgetknives.com

TYPE OF KNIFE
P'ti folding knife

LOCKING SYSTEM (FOR FOLDING KNIVES)
Frame lock

STEEL
CPM-154 CM

HANDLE MATERIAL(S)
Titanium. clip and spacer made from Mokuti

PRICE

TYPE OF KNIFE
Folding knife

LOCKING SYSTEM (FOR FOLDING KNIVES)
Liner lock

STEEL
154CM

HANDLE MATERIAL(S)
Plates, bolster, spacer and clip made from bronze anodized titanium. Lightning strike carbon fiber scales

PRICE
★★

TYPE OF KNIFE
Fif folding knife

LOCKING SYSTEM (FOR FOLDING KNIVES)
Liner lock

STEEL
CPM-154 CM on CCBearing

HANDLE MATERIAL(S)
Carbon fiber.
Titanium clip.

SIZE
201 mm (open)

PRICE
★★

TONY KARLSSON

Both a furniture restorer and knifemaker, Tony Karlsson has plenty to keep him busy during the long Swedish winters. He lives in the south of the country, in Agunnaryd, closer to Copenhagen in Denmark than it is to Stockholm. There are plenty of ways to learn about the knifemaking industry in Sweden, where there are thousands of knifemakers, most of them amateurs. To begin with, Tony specialized in Nordic-style knives with fixed blades. Little by little, he started making folding knives, to which he added traditional Nordic decorative elements. Thanks to his knowledge of woodworking, he also makes elegant cases for his creations. Tony does not do his own forging — he uses Damascus steel made by the best blacksmiths in his country, home to many famous blacksmiths: Roger Bergh, Kay Embretsen, Johan Gustavsson, the Nylund brothers. He chooses the patterns that go best with the knife he's making at the time.

www.karlssonknives.com

TYPE OF KNIFE
Folding knife

LOCKING SYSTEM (FOR FOLDING KNIVES)
Flipper

STEEL
Dragon Skin Damascus Steel (made by Bertie Rietveld - South Africa)

HANDLE MATERIAL(S)
Titanium plates, with scales and spacer made from meteorite (Muonionalusta)

SIZE
220 mm (open)

PRICE

Sweden

TYPE OF KNIFE
Folding dagger

LOCKING SYSTEM (FOR FOLDING KNIVES)
Liner lock

STEEL
Damascus stainless steel
(blade and bolsters)

HANDLE MATERIAL(S)
Engraved anodized
titanium plates and blue
mammoth ivory scales.
Custom box.

PRICE
★★★

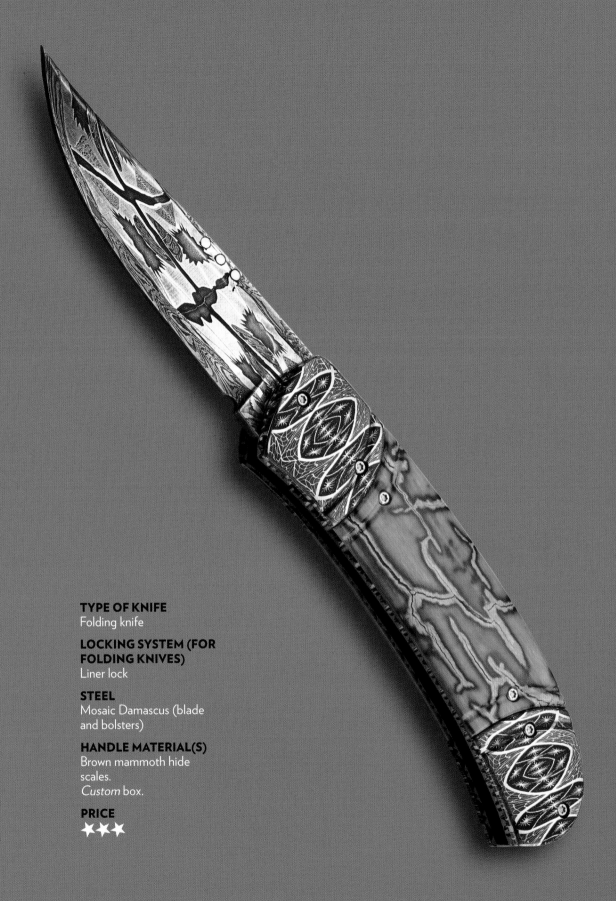

TYPE OF KNIFE
Folding knife

LOCKING SYSTEM (FOR FOLDING KNIVES)
Liner lock

STEEL
Mosaic Damascus (blade and bolsters)

HANDLE MATERIAL(S)
Brown mammoth hide scales.
Custom box.

PRICE
★ ★ ★

RON LAKE

Rightly considered one of the fathers of modern knifemaking, Ron Lake continues to innovate after 50 years of knifemaking With a degree in the field of machine tools, he started working in strategic equipment in the early 1960s, and then he worked on prototypes for the aeronautics and automobile industries. He started making knives as an amateur in 1965, primarily fixed blade hunting knives. Then he began working on a folding knife locking system which would become his famous "Trail-lock Interframe Folding knife". Change of direction: Ron became a knifemaker. In 1971, he joined the American Knifemaker's Guild. Some 50 years later, this Trail lock design remains one of the most famous in modern knifemaking history, and one of the most popular among collectors. Ron Lake designs both knives and mechanisms for the knifemaking industry and contributes to technical books and trade magazines.

The "Lake Interframe Folder" can be found in the most prestigious collections, as well as in the Smithsonian Museum and the Metal Museum in Memphis.

Ron Lake participates in the ECCKS in New York and AKI in San Diego.

www.lakeknives.com

TYPE OF KNIFE
Two Classic Interframe Backlock Folders

LOCKING SYSTEM (FOR FOLDING KNIVES)
Back lock

STEEL
ATS-34

HANDLE MATERIAL(S)
416 stainless steel with amber deer antlers (Indian sambar deer) inserts. Gold suspension rings.

SIZE
150 mm and 175 mm (open)

PRICE
★★★★

Ron Lake

OPPOSITE

TYPE OF KNIFE
Classic Interframe folding knife

LOCKING SYSTEM (FOR FOLDING KNIVES)
Back lock

STEEL
ATS-35
("parachute" blade)

HANDLE MATERIAL(S)
416 stainless steel with phenolic resin inserts and gold square and thread inlays

SIZE
246 mm (open)

PRICE
★★★★

TYPE OF KNIFE
Classic Interframe Backlock Folding knife

LOCKING SYSTEM (FOR FOLDING KNIVES)
Back lock

STEEL
ATS-34

HANDLE MATERIAL(S)
416 stainless steel with "black" mother-of-pearl inserts.
Gold toothpicks.

SIZE
150 mm (open)

PRICE
★★★★

VÉRONIQUE LAURENT

Véronique Laurent was already interested in knifemaking when she discovered forging in 2004 during a trip to the *Fête du Fer* (Ironfest), in the Paimpont forest, while on vacation in Brittany. There, many demonstrators work in front of an audience of both amateurs and connoisseurs — forging leaves an impression on everyone as there is something mysterious and magical about it. She met some great people there, and discovered that her home country, Belgium, was represented there and has a very active association of knifemakers: the Belgian Knives Society (BKS). This association offers regular blacksmithing courses, and Véronique signed up to one of them as soon as she got home: she gradually caught the bug! Many French forums have been created, including forgefr. com and the more private *Le Bar de la forge*. Some members are very charismatic. Véronique and her partner, Michel Slosse, were then invited to a "Hammer In" in Burgundy, a knifemaker-blacksmith meeting organized by Pascal "Doc" Mangenot, a pharmacist passionate about knife forging. There, they met American knifemaker Joe Keeslar and his wife, who own a home in the Morvan. Joe is the president of the American Bladesmith Society (ABS). Other American knifemakers and blacksmiths were present, and during the evening, what did they talk about? Forging, ABS, and its philosophy, which is based on sharing knowledge. The following year, the idea caught on: Véronique passed the probationary tests, then travelled to BLADE Show Atlanta to present her work before a jury of Mastersmiths. She was accepted as a Journeymam Smith in 2013. Two years later, she was awarded the honor of Mastersmith! Her partner, Michel Slosse, tailor made each of her machines, one by one. He's very talented! These included a backstand, quenching furnace, hydraulic press, forge and burner.

Her knives are most often made from multi-bar Damascus steel with a fixed blade (quite large in size), although she also makes a few folding knives. She has had a lot of success on the other side of the Atlantic, as well as in Brazil, where there is a big market for this type of knife. Fossilized ivory, mother-of-pearl and precious woods adorn her handles. She participates in the BLADE Show (where she has won several awards) at the Sao Paulo Exhibition in Brazil, and visits her knifemaker friends at the exhibitions in Gembloux and Thiers.

TYPE OF KNIFE
Keyhole folding knife

LOCKING SYSTEM (FOR FOLDING KNIVES)
Mid-lock

STEEL
Explosion Damascus

HANDLE MATERIAL(S)
Explosion Damascus and mother-of-pearl

SIZE
170 mm (open)

PRICE
★ ★

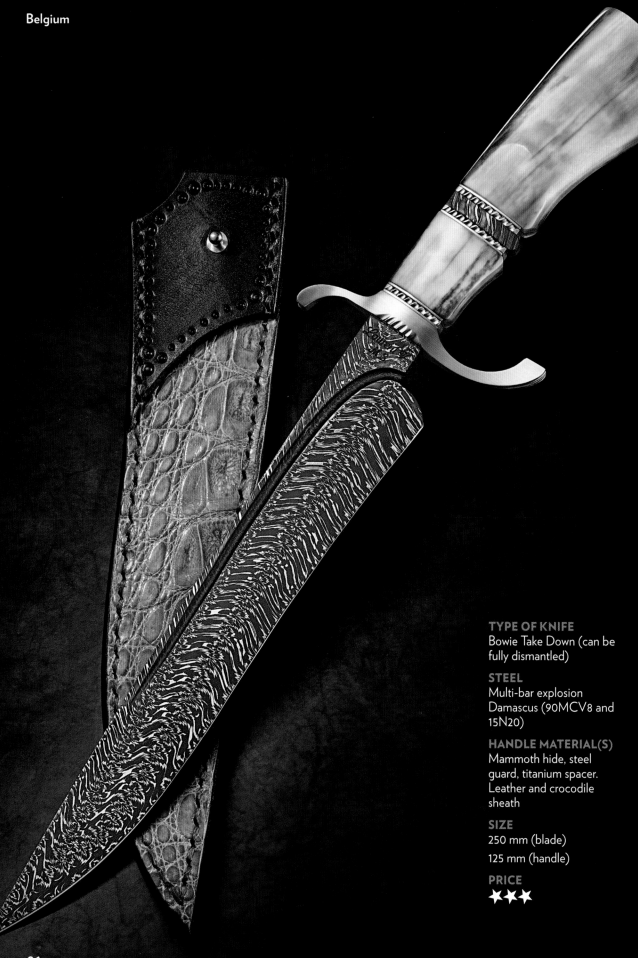

TYPE OF KNIFE
Bowie Take Down (can be fully dismantled)

STEEL
Multi-bar explosion Damascus (90MCV8 and 15N20)

HANDLE MATERIAL(S)
Mammoth hide, steel guard, titanium spacer. Leather and crocodile sheath

SIZE
250 mm (blade)
125 mm (handle)

PRICE
★★★

TYPE OF KNIFE
Small dagger

STEEL
Birdy Damascus in
90MCV8 and 15N20

HANDLE MATERIAL(S)
Steel guard and pommel,
carved ebony handle.
Leather and
shagreen sheath

SIZE
250 mm (blade)
125 mm (handle)

PRICE
★★★

Belgium

TYPE OF KNIFE
Left-handed Adrienne
dagger, can be dismantled

STEEL
Multi-bar explosion
Damascus in the center
and cutting edge added in
90MCV8

HANDLE MATERIAL(S)
Guard and ring in file-
worked steel, handle in
buffalo horn and engine-
turned titanium. Sheath in
leather and shagreen

SIZE
320 mm (blade)
140 mm (handle)

PRICE
★★★★

Véronique Laurent

DAVID LESPECT

David Lespect comes from somewhere cold... professionally, that is! His first job was in air conditioning, which he did for seven years, mainly on the Island of Réunion. When he returned to mainland France, it was through reading that he discovered there was knifemaking outside of the industrial knives he had collected since childhood. In 2005, he decided he wanted to be a knifemaker and reached out to a knifemaker-blacksmith in his region, Christian Avakian, with whom he completed a course that would have a lasting impact on him.

His parents lent him a small space in which he set up his workshop and he forged whenever he had time. He searched for his style, something some people never find. But he found it quite quickly. Think about his first knives, made about ten years ago, at the first show he attended, in Lyon, and it was obvious he already had the mark of a great knifemaker! In the years that followed, this was confirmed.

David Lespect is a gifted knifemaker, something unanimously recognized by his peers. His range is made up of semi-integral fixed blade knives and modern, classy, liner lock and frame lock folding knives, with and without flippers. He forges all his blades, as well as his own Damascus steel. He uses titanium, local and exotic countries, carbon fiber, and mammoth and warthog ivory.

David Lespect never names his knives, as they are all different and, therefore, unique: he works without a template and according to what inspires him in the moment.

He participates in the Nyons show, FICX-Paris, EKS-Strasbourg, Gembloux (Belgium), Sauclières (Larzac) and BLADE Show Atlanta.

www.davidlespect.com

TYPE OF KNIFE
Folding knife

LOCKING SYSTEM (FOR FOLDING KNIVES)
Frame lock

STEEL
Forged C105, selective quenching

HANDLE MATERIAL(S)
Titanium and deer antler

SIZE
195 mm (open)

PRICE

TYPE OF KNIFE
Davles folding knife

**LOCKING SYSTEM (FOR
FOLDING KNIVES)**
Liner lock

STEEL
Damascus steel forged by
the artist

HANDLE MATERIAL(S)
D2 "stonewashed" bolsters
and warthog ivory scales

PRICE

TYPE OF KNIFE
Persian folding knife

LOCKING SYSTEM (FOR FOLDING KNIVES)
Liner lock

STEEL
D2 "stonewashed" steel

PRICE

TYPE OF KNIFE
Semi-integral, fixed blade

STEEL
Forged 100CR6, selective quenching

HANDLE MATERIAL(S)
D2 "stonewashed" bolsters and sandblasted carbon fiber scales

SIZE
190 mm

PRICE

ELIZABETH AND WOLFGANG LOERCHNER

Wolfgang Loerchner started making knives around forty years ago. At the time, he used a few files and some sandpaper. Nowadays, not much has changed! He doesn't use many machines and believes that this gives him perfect control of his work, as well as total freedom in the design of his knives.

He mainly uses 440c steels for his knife blades and 416 for the handles, which he carves and into which he inserts Damascus steel, gold and natural materials.

Wolfgang Loerchner is a special knifemaker who makes very few knives.

He participates in AKI in San Diego, FICX-Paris and a few other exhibitions in the United States. Recently, he became involved in a new approach to tactical knives with the young company Patriot Bladewerks, for which he creates designs.

Elizabeth is Wolfgang's daughter, and she has always been immersed in her father's creative universe, even if she was destined for another type of creativity: painting, drawing, and composition. But, to our delight, she finally caught the knifemaking bug.

She says of her art: "The evidence of a new passion was obvious. The indescribable itch in my fingers, which had always been for a brush, was quickly replaced by the uncontrollable desire to pick up a file. I've never looked back." She produces classy, elegant knives with delicate, feminine shapes.

www.ecloerchner.com

TYPE OF KNIFE
Folding knife

LOCKING SYSTEM (FOR FOLDING KNIVES)
Back lock

STEEL
440C

HANDLE MATERIAL(S)
416 stainless steel with Damasteel© inserts. The sculpting is done exclusively with files and sandpaper.

PRICE
★★★

TYPE OF KNIFE
"03 flipper" folding knife

LOCKING SYSTEM (FOR FOLDING KNIVES)
Liner lock

STEEL
CPM-43

HANDLE MATERIAL(S)
Titanium

SIZE
228 mm (open)

PRICE
★★★★

TYPE OF KNIFE
Folding knife

LOCKING SYSTEM (FOR FOLDING KNIVES)
Back lock

STEEL
440C

HANDLE MATERIAL(S)
416 stainless steel with Damasteel© and mother-of-pearl inserts

PRICE
★★★★

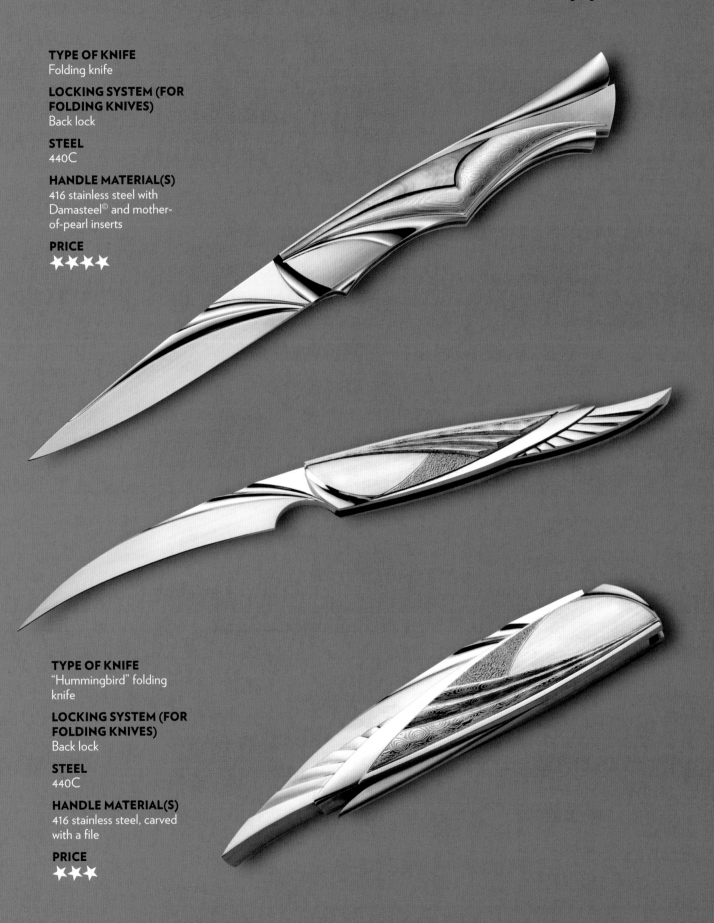

TYPE OF KNIFE
"Hummingbird" folding knife

LOCKING SYSTEM (FOR FOLDING KNIVES)
Back lock

STEEL
440C

HANDLE MATERIAL(S)
416 stainless steel, carved with a file

PRICE
★★★

THOMAS AND CLAES LÖFGREN

Thomas (father) and Claes (son) Löfgren often work together, although they both produce a few individual creations. They are very active members of the Swedish Knife Association (Svensk Knivförening), in which they contribute towards training new knifemakers, in the form of courses on knife handle fabrication, as well as that of traditional Nordic sheaths (*pauting*: leather molding technique). As with many Swedish knifemakers, they do not do their own forging. For their knife blades, they use Damascus steel made by the top Scandinavian specialists. They only make fixed-blade knives in a purely Scandinavian style, inspired by traditional Nordic knife designs, for which they use precious and rare materials found in the far North, such as fossilized walrus and mammoth ivory, stabilized and colored mammoth molar, musk ox horn, silicified bogwood, stabilized birch burl, etc.

They sometimes present their work at international shows in Sweden, Finland (Helsinki), the United States and France (FICX-Paris and Coutellia in Thiers).

TYPE OF KNIFE
Phoenix Dagger, fixed blade

STEEL
Damascus steel by Roger Bergh (Sweden)

HANDLE MATERIAL(S)
Mammoth ivory, bronze elements (Nylund forge) and Damascus steel

PRICE
★★★★

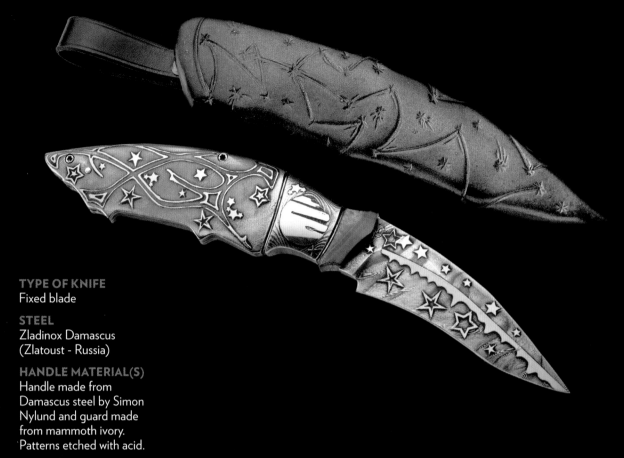

TYPE OF KNIFE
Fixed blade

STEEL
Zladinox Damascus
(Zlatoust - Russia)

HANDLE MATERIAL(S)
Handle made from
Damascus steel by Simon
Nylund and guard made
from mammoth ivory.
Patterns etched with acid.

PRICE
★★

TYPE OF KNIFE
Fixed blade

STEEL
Damascus (forged by the
Nylund brothers - Finland)

HANDLE MATERIAL(S)
Mammoth ivory and teeth,
bronze, and nickel silver

PRICE
★★

TYPE OF KNIFE
Fixed blade

STEEL
Mosaic Damascus by
Johan Gustavsson

HANDLE MATERIAL(S)
Mammoth ivory and molar,
stained and stabilized
fossilized walrus teeth

PRICE
★★

SAMUEL LURQUIN

Samuel Lurquin lives in Binche, in the Belgian province of Hainaut, where he is a dog handler by trade; this is his first passion, the second being forging and knifemaking. Or perhaps it is the other way around...

He is a gentle giant, with a strong sense of community and sharing, values that he finds in members of the American Bladesmith Society, of which he has become one of the few European Mastersmiths. His motto is: "As if my life depended on it!" This phrase just about says it all, and is in line with the concept some of his friends have of knifemaking: it's like a philosophy! He's a tool manufacturer, and will remain one. But he is no stranger to aesthetic criteria, and his knives have a rugged beauty.

Fixed blade knives, made with W2- or Damascus steel-forged blades. He has not produced any folding knives yet, but he has designed some with Tashi Bharucha and David Lespect. He studies all factors, from metallurgy (heat treatment) to the tipping point to provide a dependable and functional tool for a specific use.

Every year, Sam participates in BLADE Show Atlanta, FICX-Paris, and the Gembloux show.

www.samuel-lurquin.com

TYPE OF KNIFE
Fighter Bowie

STEEL
W2 forged

HANDLE MATERIAL(S)
Steel guard, stabilized Koa handle

SHEATH
Sheath by Aaron Sybrant

PRICE
★★★

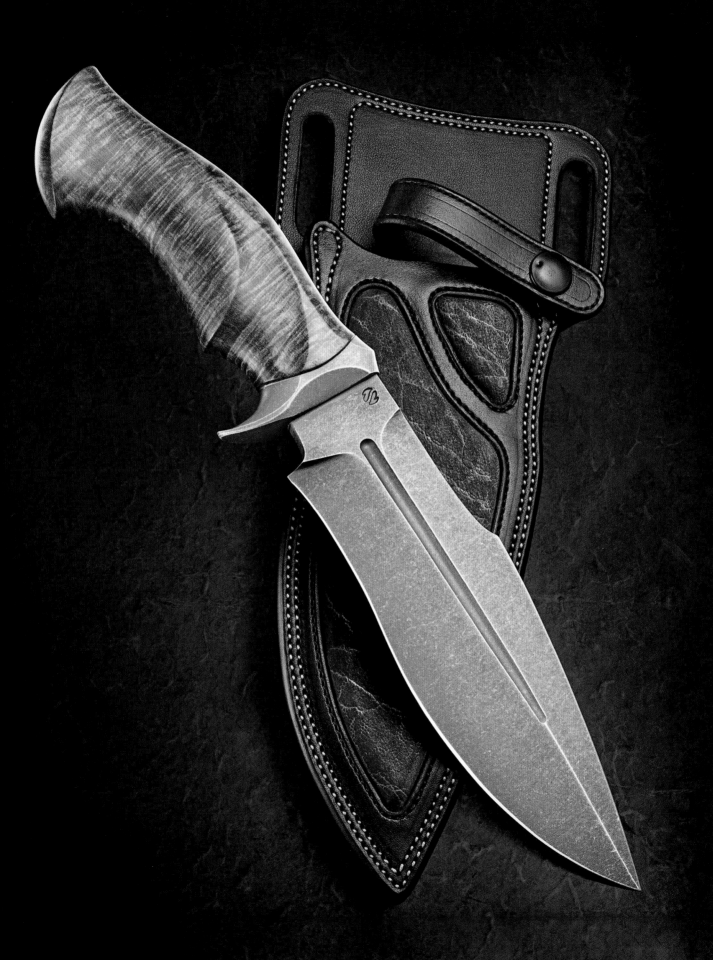

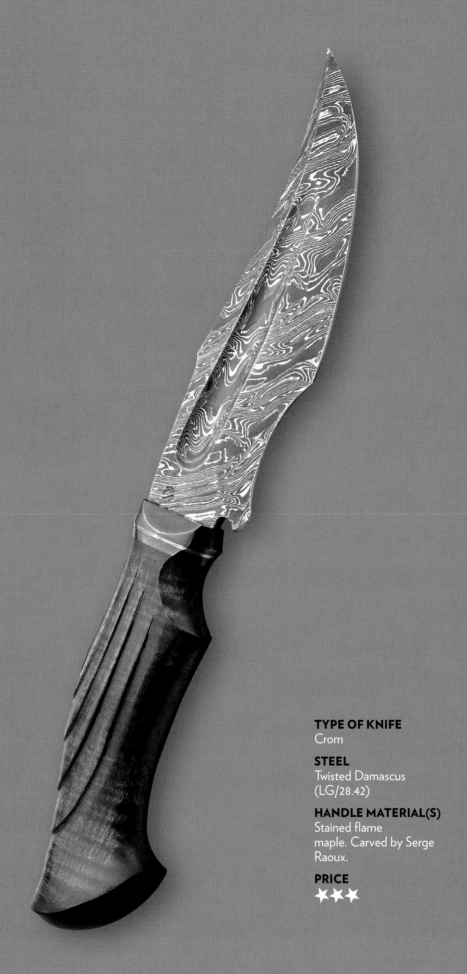

TYPE OF KNIFE
Crom

STEEL
Twisted Damascus
(LG/28.42)

HANDLE MATERIAL(S)
Stained flame
maple. Carved by Serge
Raoux.

PRICE
★★★

TYPE OF KNIFE
Semi-integral

STEEL
W2 forged, parkerized
finish

HANDLE MATERIAL(S)
Carved G10 by Serge
Raoux

PRICE

ANDREW MEERS

Originally from Boston, Andrew Meers has a degree in sculpture (Massachusetts College of Art and Design in Boston) and forging/metallurgy (Southern Illinois University in Carbondale). He was also an artist-in-residence at the National Ornamental Metal Museum. He lives in Memphis, Tennessee. A member of the American Bladesmith Society, he became a Journeyman Smith in 2013 and Mastersmith in 2015. He was also given the B.R. Hughes Award.

His creativity is not limited to knifemaking; he is interested in objects and shapes, metalwork in general, and Japanese metalwork in particular, from which he draws inspiration to decorate his knives.

Andrew also occasionally teaches a master class at the Penland School of Arts and Crafts in North Carolina.

Andrew Meers is an artist of his time, influenced by his Asian origins.

He showcases his work at the BLADE Show and particularly enjoyed his involvement in FICX and his stay in Paris.

www.instagram.com/mr.meers

TYPE OF KNIFE
Bumblebee folding knife

LOCKING SYSTEM (FOR FOLDING KNIVES)
Liner lock

STEEL
Damascus (1084/15N20)

HANDLE MATERIAL(S)
Steel with gold, silver, mokume-gane and ruby inlays. Bee and flower patterns.

SIZE
184 mm (open)

PRICE
★★★

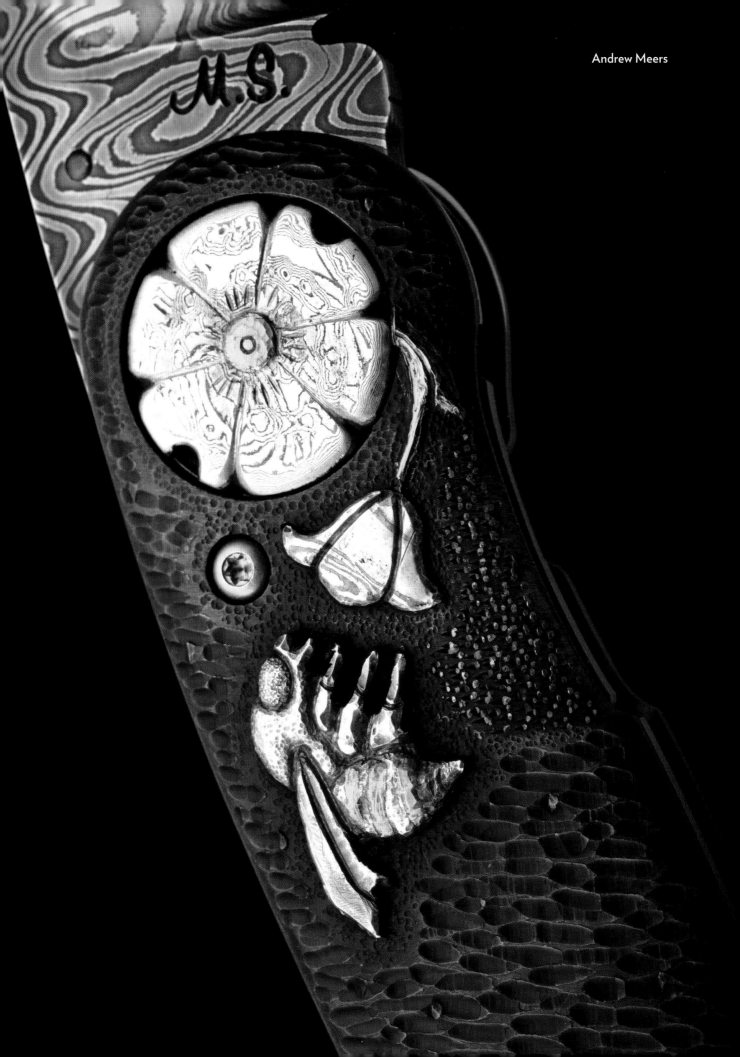

Andrew Meers

TYPE OF KNIFE
Black Dagger

STEEL
"Chevron" Damascus

HANDLE MATERIAL(S)
Guard and pommel made
from twisted Damascus and
fluted ebony with a twisted
silver thread inlay. Ladybug
inlay on the guard.

PRICE
★★★

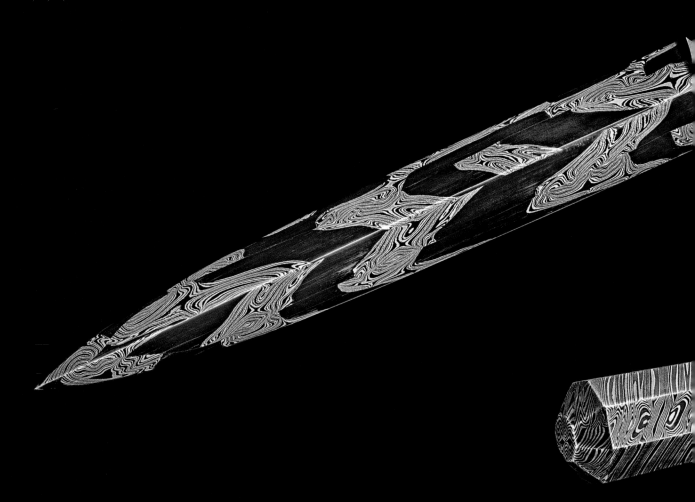

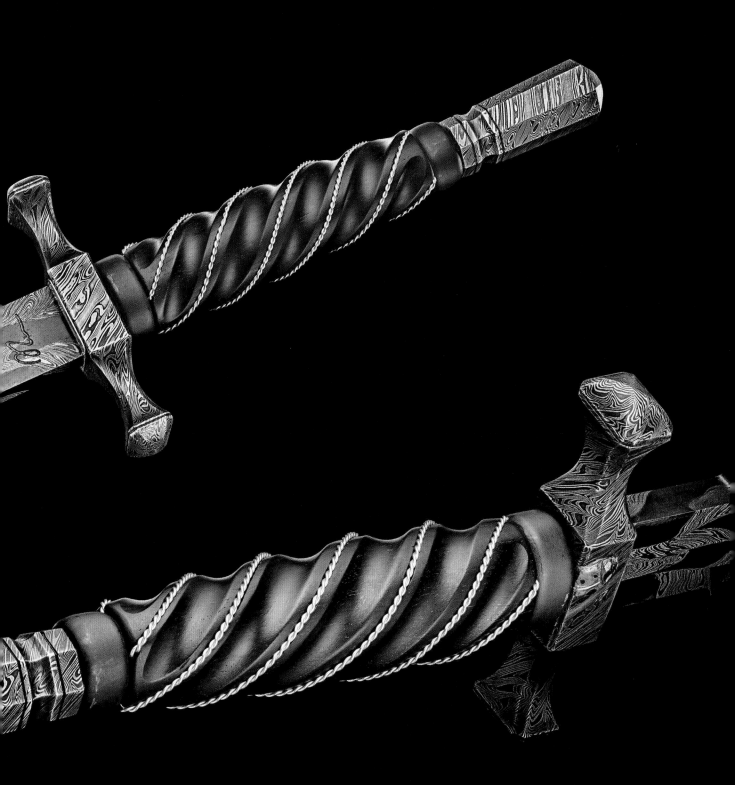

TYPE OF KNIFE
Folding Eagle knife

LOCKING SYSTEM (FOR FOLDING KNIVES)
Liner lock

STEEL
Damascus, complex grind

HANDLE MATERIAL(S)
Scratched steel with concealed yellow mother-of-pearl inserts

SIZE
203 mm (open)

PRICE
★ ★ ★

Andrew Meers

TYPE OF KNIFE
Semi-integral fixed blade

STEEL
Damascus wave, with a
complex grind

HANDLE MATERIAL(S)
"Keyhole" assembly,
Damascus and stained
maple

PRICE
★★★

MICKAËL MOING

Mickaël Moing is part of the new generation of French artisan knifemakers. His workshop is based in Saint-Privat d'Allier (43580), not far from Puy-en-Velay.

As a graduate with a *Brevet de Technicien Supérieur* (French two-year professional degree) in agriculture, he first worked rearing goats in Brittany. Homesickness led him to return to Auvergne, where he quickly became a full-time knifemaker, blacksmith and sculptor. His knives are created between a hammer and anvil. He makes his own Damascus steel (simple and complex: mosaic, explosion, twisted, etc.) and adorns some of his creations with animal sculptures.

Most of his works are single pieces, folding or fixed blade knives; from the miniature knife to the enormous Bowie (which he humorously renamed "Growie"). He participates in the two most popular French exhibitions: Coutellia, in Thiers, and the *Fête du Couteau* (Knife Festival) in Nontron, Périgord. For the rest of the year, he mainly sells his good on his website. In 2019, for the first time, he participated in the largest knifemaking show in the world: BLADE Show Atlanta (Georgia, United States).

Knifemaking is a way to express himself, which he takes great pleasure. He describes it as: "One of the few activities which allows you to work with metal, wood, leather and many other materials. It has no limits."

www.couteaux-moing.com

TYPE OF KNIFE
Pair of Zigs

LOCKING SYSTEM (FOR FOLDING KNIVES)
Integral slipjoint

STEEL
XC-75

HANDLE MATERIAL(S)
Folded XC-75 sheet steel and mammoth ivory scales

SIZE
180 mm and 130 mm (open)

PRICE
★

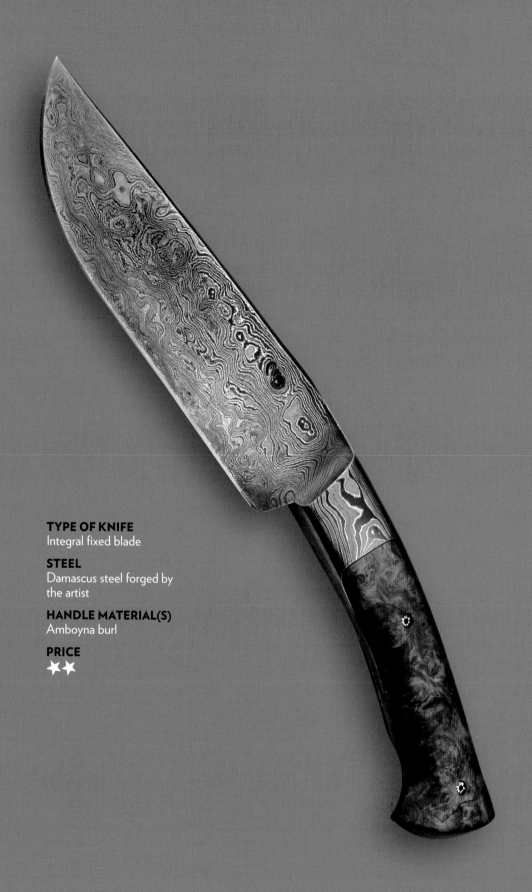

TYPE OF KNIFE
Integral fixed blade

STEEL
Damascus steel forged by
the artist

HANDLE MATERIAL(S)
Amboyna burl

PRICE
★ ★

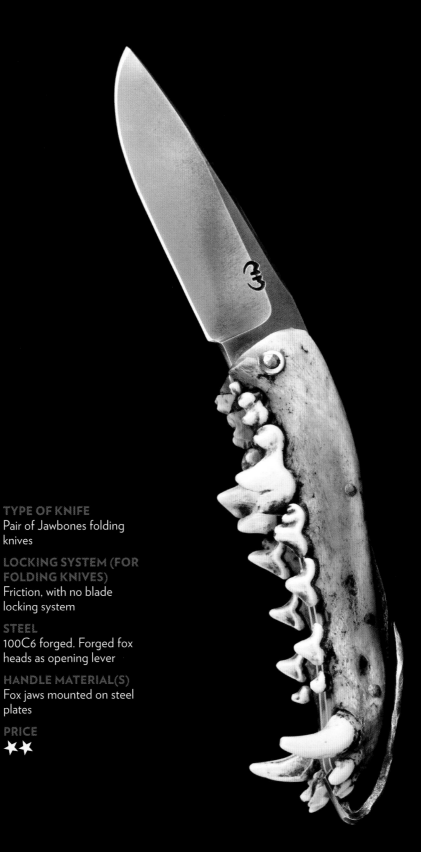

TYPE OF KNIFE
Pair of Jawbones folding knives

LOCKING SYSTEM (FOR FOLDING KNIVES)
Friction, with no blade locking system

STEEL
100C6 forged. Forged fox heads as opening lever

HANDLE MATERIAL(S)
Fox jaws mounted on steel plates

PRICE
★★

CORRADO MORO

At the beginning of his knifemaking career, Corrado Moro designed many models for other people. Then he started to do it for himself.

He was born in Turin, in 1972, where he completed his studies in precision engineering. He worked for 23 years as a tool-maker and digital control specialist. At the same time, he built a small workshop where he developed various projects related to his profession, including several knives. In 2012, after having participated in the exhibition in Burgundy, he was invited to attend the prestigious New York exhibition. On his return to Italy, he decided to become a full-time knifemaker.

He enjoys innovation, rule-breaking, and finding new solutions. He draws his inspiration from everyday life, from nature, the animal world, mechanics, motorcycles and racing machines, aeronautics... Not to mention watches and their intricacies!

www.moroknives.com

TYPE OF KNIFE
Infinity Prototype folding knife, inspired by the world of motorcycling

LOCKING SYSTEM (FOR FOLDING KNIVES)
Twin lock, on ball bearings

STEEL
RWL-34 RSP

HANDLE MATERIAL(S)
416 stainless steel, titanium, and pearl oyster mother-of-pearl

SIZE
211 mm (open)
96 mm (closed)

PRICE
★★★

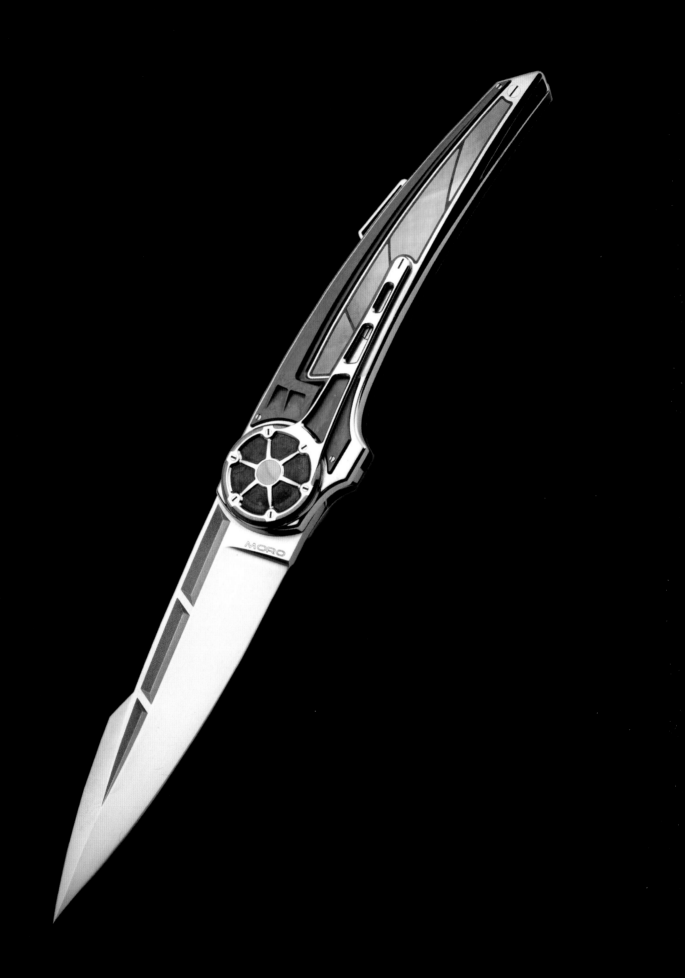

TYPE OF KNIFE
Folding dagger
Desmo Blue Arrow

LOCKING SYSTEM (FOR FOLDING KNIVES)
Desmo lock, on ball bearings

STEEL
RWL-34 RSP

HANDLE MATERIAL(S)
416 stainless steel, mother-of-pearl, carbon fiber, titanium and gold

SIZE
220 mm (open)
97 mm (closed)

PRICE
★★★★

TYPE OF KNIFE
Tourbillon Mignon folding knife, inspired by the famous intricate watches of the same name.

LOCKING SYSTEM (FOR FOLDING KNIVES)
Mid-lock

STEEL
RWL-34 RSP

HANDLE MATERIAL(S)
416 stainless steel inserts made from rose and yellow gold

SIZE
155 mm (open)
89 mm (closed)

PRICE
★★★★

TYPE OF KNIFE
Skynet folding dagger

LOCKING SYSTEM (FOR FOLDING KNIVES)
Twin lock, on ball bearings

STEEL
RWL-34 RSP

HANDLE MATERIAL(S)
416 stainless steel with Damascus steel inserts

SIZE
207 mm (open)
92 mm (closed)

PRICE
★★★★

HIDETOSHI NAKAYAMA

Hidetoshi Nakayama entered the world of knifemaking in a roundabout way, working in the after-sales-service and sharpening department at a reputable knifemaking company in Tokyo. In 1989, he joined the workshop of Noboyuki Uekama, a very highly respected artisan in Japan. He perfected his knowledge with master Yasufusa Saito, who taught him about the subtleties of the art of *netsuke*, clothing accessories in the form of small carved items, designed to be attached as "hanging objects" on belts (sagemono).

In 2000, Hidetoshi became a fine art knifemaker in Yokohama, a big port town close to Tokyo. He combines everything he has learnt from master knifemakers and sculptors into his knives. His pieces are very delicate, truly poetic.

Hidetoshi produces few pieces and some of his knives take two weeks to three months of work. There are perhaps fifteen knives carved per year, to which he adds silver objects (pendants and netsuke) and a range of pens with a particular mechanism.

His favorite patterns include fake bamboo, sea creatures, lizards and other geckos, and cats, to which he adds demons and dragons, rich in Japanese mythology.

Hidetoshi Nakayama's knives take us on a journey through a universe where the wondrous and fantastical go hand in hand with the poetical.

TYPE OF KNIFE
Higonokami style folding knife, inspired by To-shu, calligraphy knife designed to erase writing errors

LOCKING SYSTEM (FOR FOLDING KNIVES)
Friction, with no blade locking system

STEEL
Shirogami

HANDLE MATERIAL(S)
Hardened steel carved to look like bamboo, with additional carving

PRICE
★★

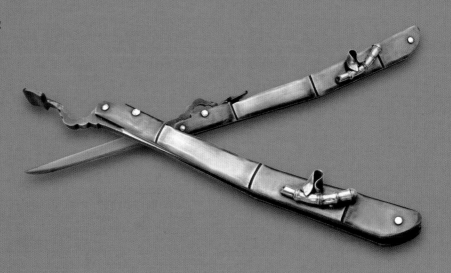

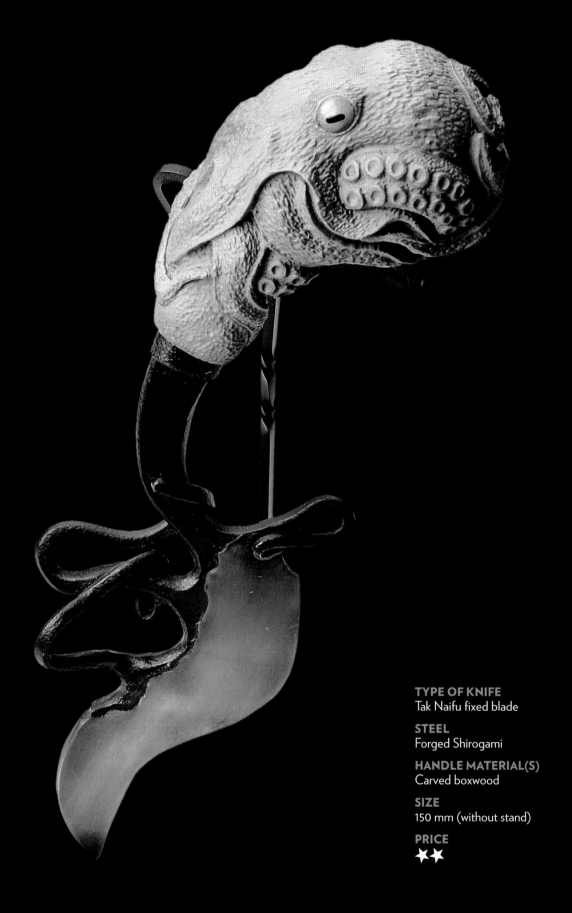

TYPE OF KNIFE
Tak Naifu fixed blade

STEEL
Forged Shirogami

HANDLE MATERIAL(S)
Carved boxwood

SIZE
150 mm (without stand)

PRICE
★★

TYPE OF KNIFE
Hornet fixed blade

STEEL
D2

HANDLE MATERIAL(S)
Nickel silver guard and
carved boxwood handle
(hornet). Sheath made
from rosewood.

SIZE
210 mm

PRICE
★★

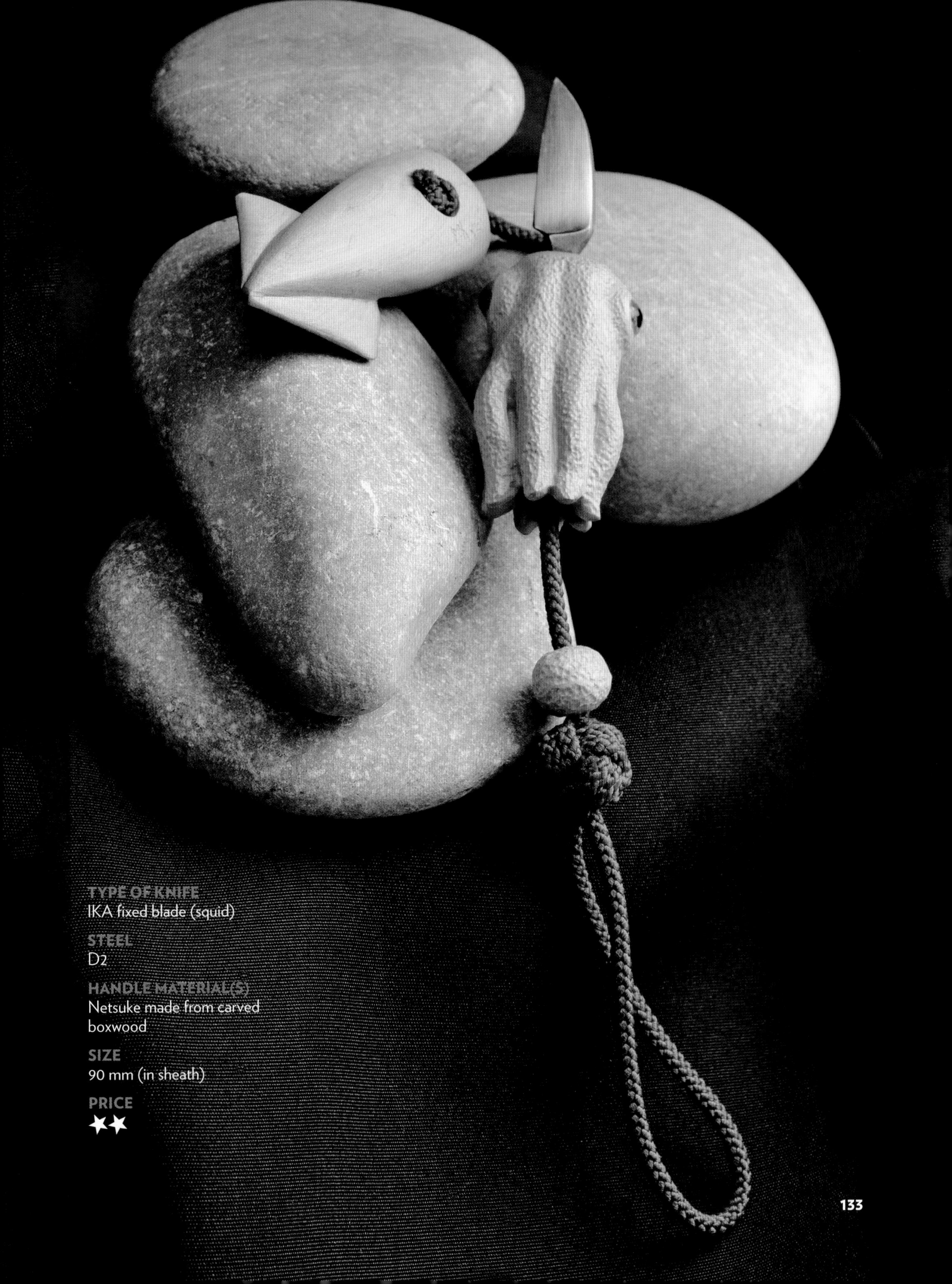

TYPE OF KNIFE
IKA fixed blade (squid)

STEEL
D2

HANDLE MATERIAL(S)
Netsuke made from carved
boxwood

SIZE
90 mm (in sheath)

PRICE
★★

SIMON AND JAKOB NYLUND

They are two young brothers: Simon, born in 1992 and Jakob, born in 1989. Their interest in knifemaking began during their teenage years. They took the plunge in 2011, making the decision to become full-time cutlers.

They make their own Damascus steel, which they also provide to their fellow knifemakers. They make their own knives, both fixed blades in the traditional Nordic style and folding blades in a much more contemporary style. While they often work on joint projects, they also produce their own individual creations, for which they do each step themselves: forging, assembly, and making any sheaths or cases.

They define their knives as ordinary yet beautiful, but it must be said that they are increasingly luxurious. Collectors snap them up and, alas, they often end up behind shop windows.

It's a shame, because their knives are forged and designed to be used, like the knives presented on these pages.

In addition to their remarkable, complex and often heat-colored Damascus steel, they use precious materials such as mammoth teeth, fossilized ivories and reindeer antlers engraved with Scandinavian patterns.

Simon and Jakob Nylund are constantly looking for new challenges, new techniques and new ways to express their art.

So far, they're doing it admirably.

They participate in shows in Helsinki, New York and at FICX-Paris.

www.facebook.com/Nylund-Knives-334084986706016/

TYPE OF KNIFE
Folding knife

LOCKING SYSTEM (FOR FOLDING KNIVES)
Back lock

STEEL
Composite - forged stainless Damascus

HANDLE MATERIAL(S)
Body made from 416 stainless steel with marbled carbon fiber inserts

PRICE
★★★

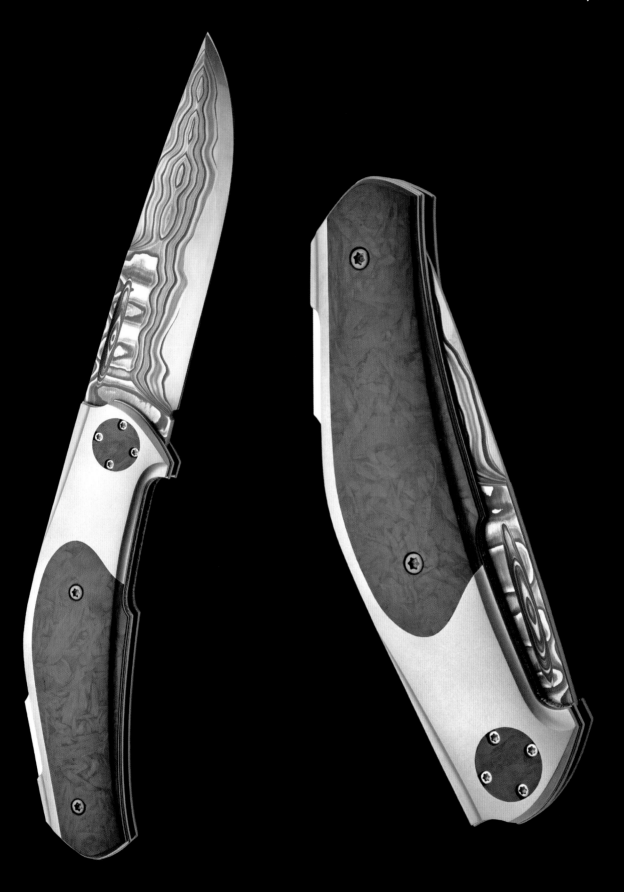

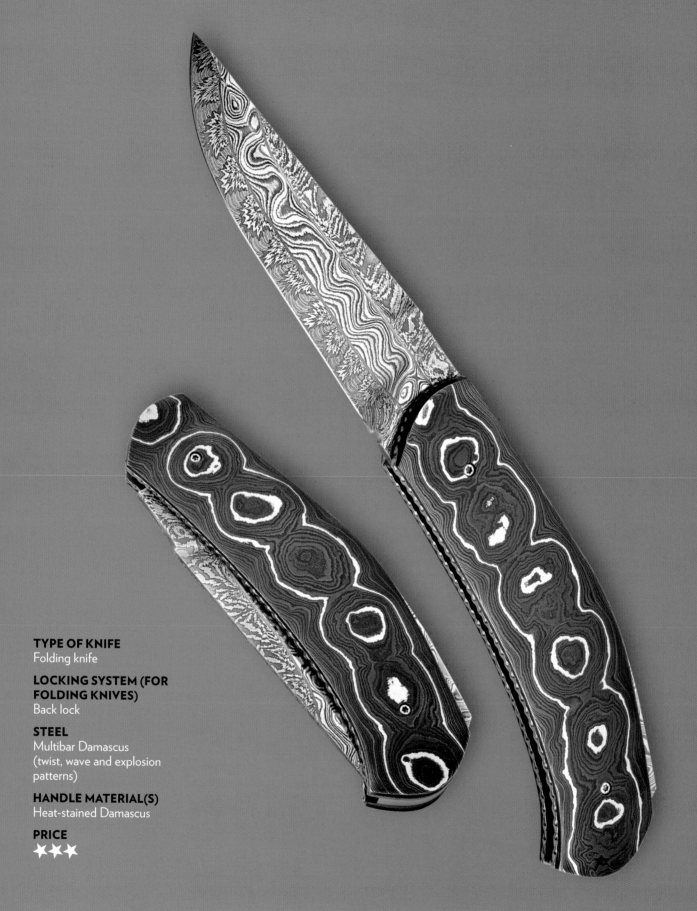

TYPE OF KNIFE
Folding knife

LOCKING SYSTEM (FOR FOLDING KNIVES)
Back lock

STEEL
Multibar Damascus
(twist, wave and explosion
patterns)

HANDLE MATERIAL(S)
Heat-stained Damascus

PRICE
★★★

TYPE OF KNIFE
Folding knife

LOCKING SYSTEM (FOR FOLDING KNIVES)
Back lock

STEEL
Composite - RWL-34 core and sides made from heat-colored nickel Damascus

HANDLE MATERIAL(S)
Steel and anodized titanium plates, heat-colored Damascus inserts

PRICE
★★★

TYPE OF KNIFE
Folding knife

LOCKING SYSTEM (FOR FOLDING KNIVES)
Back lock

STEEL
Composite - RWL-34 core and sides made from heat-colored nickel Damascus

HANDLE MATERIAL(S)
Heat-colored Damascus with engraved copper inserts by Chantal Schaschl (Austria).
Birch burl box.

PRICE

CHRISTIAN PENOT

There's life after trains! This is what Christian Penot might say, after having started his career working for the RATP Group (Parisian public transit authority) as a train conductor.

Completely self-taught and very skillful with his hands, he started by building his own house, then he made his furniture, and lastly, he built his workshop.

The idea to make knives came to him when he was quite young: he was brought up in the countryside and has a very close relationship with nature — he is also a well-known wildlife photographer. Due to his methodical nature, he went to train in Thiers with Jean-Pierre Veysseyre, a specialist in Damascus steel. With this material, the creative possibilities are endless and he creates many patterns. Each forging session is a new adventure.

He can make very traditional knives, such as those in his regional French set. But he also enjoys creating new folding knife models, in which he combines the complexity of Damascus steel with the natural beauty of semi-precious stones, which he incorporates into the design.

Some of his models are classically carved while others are distinctly modern, with inserts made from synthetic materials like carbon fiber. He has also tried his hand at automatic opening knives.

Nothing scares Christian Penot, who enjoys a challenge (he digitized his milling machine himself). He truly makes a wide range of knives.

He shows his work at exhibitions in Nontron (Périgord), FICX-Paris, and Coutellia (Thiers).

http://couteauxpenot.free.fr

TYPE OF KNIFE
Scarab beetle folding knife

LOCKING SYSTEM (FOR FOLDING KNIVES)
Liner lock

STEEL
Ladder Damascus

HANDLE MATERIAL(S)
Mosaic Damascus bolster, dyed mammoth tooth scales

PRICE

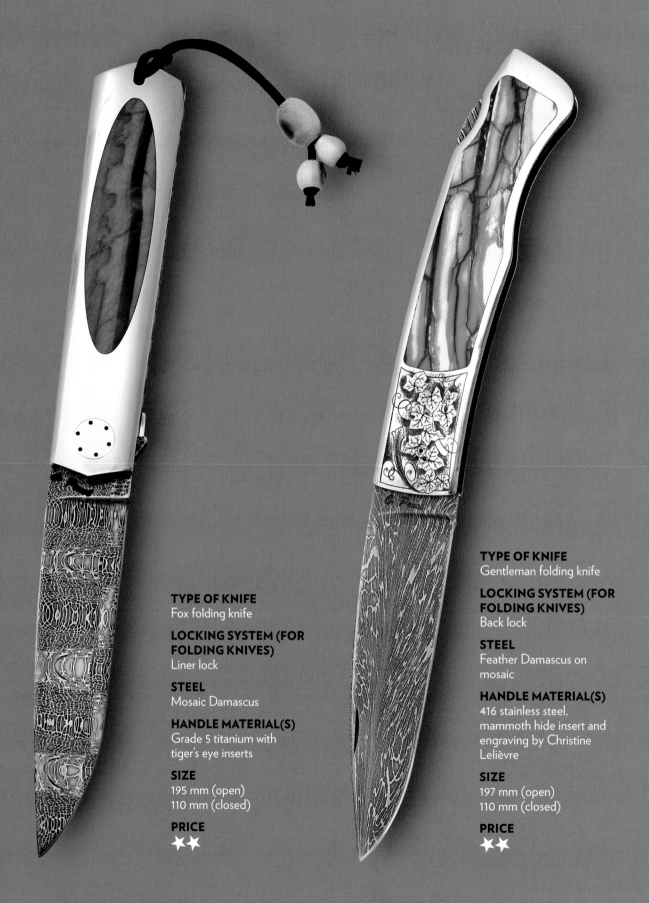

TYPE OF KNIFE
Fox folding knife

LOCKING SYSTEM (FOR FOLDING KNIVES)
Liner lock

STEEL
Mosaic Damascus

HANDLE MATERIAL(S)
Grade 5 titanium with tiger's eye inserts

SIZE
195 mm (open)
110 mm (closed)

PRICE
★★

TYPE OF KNIFE
Gentleman folding knife

LOCKING SYSTEM (FOR FOLDING KNIVES)
Back lock

STEEL
Feather Damascus on mosaic

HANDLE MATERIAL(S)
416 stainless steel, mammoth hide insert and engraving by Christine Lelièvre

SIZE
197 mm (open)
110 mm (closed)

PRICE
★★

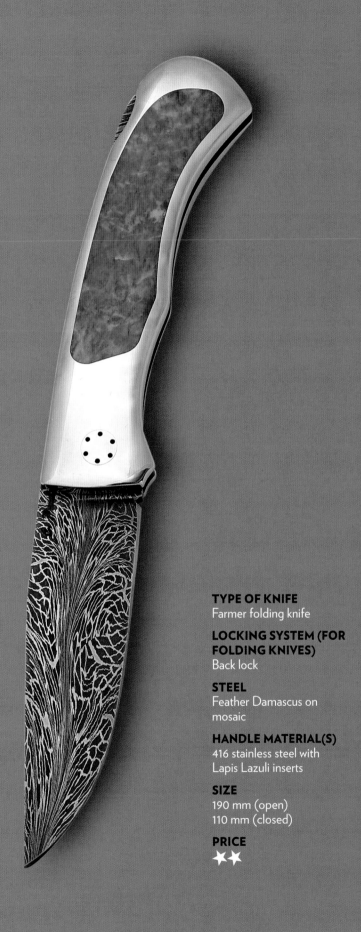

TYPE OF KNIFE
Farmer folding knife

LOCKING SYSTEM (FOR FOLDING KNIVES)
Back lock

STEEL
Feather Damascus on mosaic

HANDLE MATERIAL(S)
416 stainless steel with Lapis Lazuli inserts

SIZE
190 mm (open)
110 mm (closed)

PRICE
★★

ERIC PLAZEN

TYPE OF KNIFE
Roselli style fixed blades

STEEL
Composite steel (three-layer: antique iron/C130/antique iron)

HANDLE MATERIAL(S)
From left to right, elm burl, thurifer juniper, and birch bramble. Forged ferrule for all three knives.

SIZE
195 mm (total)

PRICE
★★

Eric Plazen made his first forged knives in the late 1980s.

Born in Paris in 1960, he moved to Toulouse in 1979 and completed a metal-working course with the A.F.P.A (adult vocational training program) during which he got to know more about forging. He discovered *La Passion des Couteaux* (Passion for Knives) magazine, which had a huge impact on him.

Eric did a lot of experimentation with steel and chose a fabrication method that would be the foundation for his future reputation: Scandinavian-style, three-layer composite steel - a layer of thick, hard steel welded between two exterior layers of soft steel.

From 1993 to 1996, he managed a bar in Saint-Girons, in the Ariège region of France, and had no time to forge. When the bar closed, he thought seriously about setting up a workshop. And he did. His first knives were sold at the outdoor market in Saint-Girons, where he spent more time explaining what his pieces were than selling them! He developed and perfected his style: simple knives, with handles made from local wood; rather Nordic in style, but with a "Japanese style" hammered iron ferrule; a composite forged blade, with a very hard steel core; a continuous tang, with rivets on the end. And he never deviates from this, or almost never. In 2002, he registered with the *Chambre des Métiers* (Chamber of Trades) as a micro-entrepreneur. Eric Plazen became a leading specialist in France and Europe in composite steels with two, three, and sometimes five layers, with a core made from hypereu-tectoid steels (with carbon percentage between 0.8% and 2.1%).

Was he the best in this field? He was not only an excellent metallurgist, self-taught and empirical, but also a remarkable knifemaker, very dedicated to a fundamental idea (when it comes to cutting, which is not necessarily what all knives are made for): obtaining the best possible blade geometry. He opted for a flat grind with an ogival finish (slightly convex).

In short, he undoubtedly made the best knives and tools with fixed blades you could dream of, knives with no fuss, just a wonderful and simple elegance.

Sadly, Eric Plazen passed away on September 26, 2015, and he is greatly missed.

France

TYPE OF KNIFE
Fixed blade "branch" knife

STEEL
Composite steel (three-layer: antique iron/C130/antique iron)

HANDLE MATERIAL(S)
Buckthorn branch

SIZE
170 mm (total), 65 mm (blade)

PRICE

France

146

TYPE OF KNIFE
Fixed blade

STEEL
Composite steel (three-layer: antique iron/145SC/antique iron)

HANDLE MATERIAL(S)
Oak from the floor of an 18th century church

SIZE
225 mm (total)

PRICE
★★

147

JEAN-LOUIS REGEL

TYPE OF KNIFE
Two Bowies, can be
dismantled

STEEL
Twisted and explosion
multi-bar Damascus (left),
wootz (right)

HANDLE MATERIAL(S)
Mammoth ivory (left)
and fossilized walrus ivory
(right).
Guard and pommel
engraved with gold thread
(left) and blued steel and
gold (right)

SIZE
415 mm (blade 270 mm)
and 430 mm (blade 300
mm)

PRICE

Jean-Louis Regel's first contact with knives was when he was very young, on his home island of Réunion, where cutting tools are used on a daily basis.

After completing a professional degree (baccalaureate) in carpentry, he gravitated towards high-level sports and moved to mainland France to get a state certificate in gymnastics, in Lorraine, far from the sun of the tropics. He travelled a lot, and it was in Thailand that he discovered forging... and that was that!

From then on, he became a bookworm and scoured Internet forums, where he discovered a "magical" steel, wootz, and his mission to master this material would become his quest for the Grail. In short, it is a crucible steel with a crystalline structure. This technique was known in India before modern times and allowed steels with a very high carbon content to be achieved.

At the same time, he started working on forging all the hardest steels. He progressed quickly, thanks to a number of highly important encounters with other experts: the German metallurgist Achim Wirtz, the French knifemaker Eric Plazen, and a Belgian couple, well-known in knifemaking circles: Véronique Laurent and Michael Slosse (she is a knifemaker, and he a bit of a mad scientist).

In 2010, he met American blacksmith Joe Keeslar, then president of the American Bladesmith Society, at a blacksmith's meeting at Pascal "Doc" Mangenot's home, in Burgundy. Friendships were formed, steps were taken and Jean-Louis, together with Véronique Laurent, embarked on an American adventure and they both became members of the ABS as Journeyman Smiths, then two years later, as Mastersmiths. They live very close to one another and progressed together, he in his workshop in Burgundy, and she in Brussels.

Jean-Louis Regel now participates in BLADE Show Atlanta and the Gembloux (Belgium) exhibition every year. He has also had great success in Brazil, where he participates in the São Paulo show.

He makes masterful pieces with complex Damascus or wootz blades, mainly large Bowie knives and daggers.

www.jeanlouis-knives.com

Jean-Louis
M.S
"Trinity"

TYPE OF KNIFE
Trinity Take Down Bowie
(can be completely
dismantled)

STEEL
Stainless wootz (crucible
steel)

HANDLE MATERIAL(S)
Warthog tooth. Guard
and pommel in "war black"
bronzed iron with 24 karat
gold inlay.

SIZE
250 mm (blade), 380 mm
(total)

PRICE
★★★

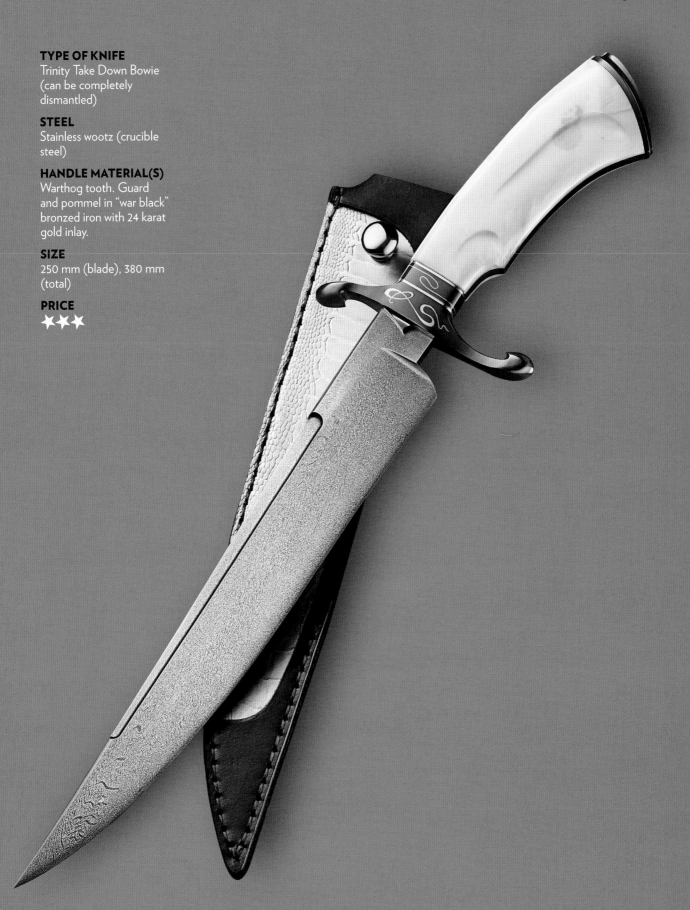

OPPOSITE

TYPE OF KNIFE
Art Nouveau dagger

STEEL
Multi-bar Damascus

HANDLE MATERIAL(S)
Water buffalo horn carved
to look like draped fabric.
Guard, clip and pommel
carved in an Art Nouveau
style

SIZE
330 mm (blade), 460 mm
(total)

PRICE

TYPE OF KNIFE
Dagger

STEEL
Multi-bar Damascus with
feather Damascus in the
middle and explosion on
the edges

HANDLE MATERIAL(S)
Ebony with silver pins.
Pommel, guard and body
with 24 karat gold inlays.
Blue shagreen sheath with
nickel silver embellishments

SIZE
330 mm (blade)

PRICE

NICOLE AND PIERRE REVERDY

Born in 1960, Pierre Reverdy completed a CAP-BEP (professional vocational qualification) in metal construction. This was followed by six years with the *Compagnons du Devoir* (French association of craftspeople and artisans), as an *Ouvrier Hautement Qualifié* (Highly Qualified Craftsman), a status he achieved in 1985 after the traditional Tour de France. He then went to England to perfect his decorative forging, and attended several international conferences on forging in France, Germany and the United States, where he stayed for several months, touring well-known blacksmith's workshops, such as Daryl Meier's. Along with his wife Nicole, he built a workshop in Valence (Drôme) in 1989, after which they moved to Romans and created the Nicole and Pierre Reverdy workshop (1999). We can thank them for many artistic creations, such as the famous "Âme Liberté" dagger which, after two centuries, revived the Damascus fabrication processes developed by Jean-François Clouet, the great French knifemaker of the 18th century. Pierre Reverdy has been a member of the *Grands Ateliers de France* (elite association for craftspeople) since 1997. In 2004, he received the title of *Maître d'art* (Master of Art), awarded by the Minister of Culture himself. Pierre Reverdy is the creator of "Poetic Damascus Steel", which he makes on his electrical discharge machine. Each pattern can take several weeks of work to complete.

The works of Pierre Reverdy are among the most famous of modern daggers: "Âme Liberté" (Free Spirit), "Volupté" (Delight), "Combat de la matière" (Material war), "Holland & Holland", "Vuitton" or "Brocatelle", "Les Roses" (Roses) (Solingen Museum), "Chœur d'étoile" (Choir of Stars), "Les Monstres" (Monsters), "Mer" (Sea), etc.

The couple also has joint works under their belt, in which they have combined Pierre's "poetic Damascus" steel and Nicole's enamels: "Fusion de 2" (Joining of 2), "Planet'Terre" (Plant Earth), the two "Vendanges" (Grape harvests), "Père Noël" (Santa Claus) and the book "Ouroboros", as well as the magnificent sword with the same name.

Pierre Reverdy has made several academicians' swords.

Pierre Reverdy participates in the Knife and Life show in Taipei, FICX-Paris and the Art Knife Invitational in San Diego.

www.reverdy.com

TYPE OF KNIFE
Pirolles folding knife (Taiwan blue magpie)

STEEL
Poetic Damascus, with a blue magpie and flower pattern

HANDLE MATERIAL(S)
Enamel by Nicole Reverdy

PRICE
★★★★

TYPE OF KNIFE
Scarface folding knife

STEEL
"Poetic" Damascus

HANDLE MATERIAL(S)
Stabilized giraffe bone with
an enamel insert by Nicole
Reverdy

SIZE
200 mm (open)

PRICE

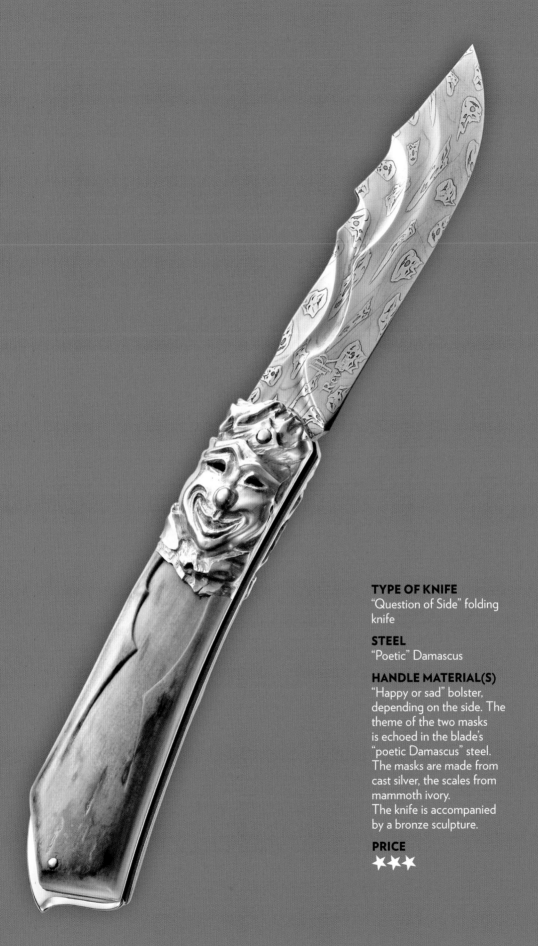

TYPE OF KNIFE
"Question of Side" folding
knife

STEEL
"Poetic" Damascus

HANDLE MATERIAL(S)
"Happy or sad" bolster,
depending on the side. The
theme of the two masks
is echoed in the blade's
"poetic Damascus" steel.
The masks are made from
cast silver, the scales from
mammoth ivory.
The knife is accompanied
by a bronze sculpture.

PRICE
★★★

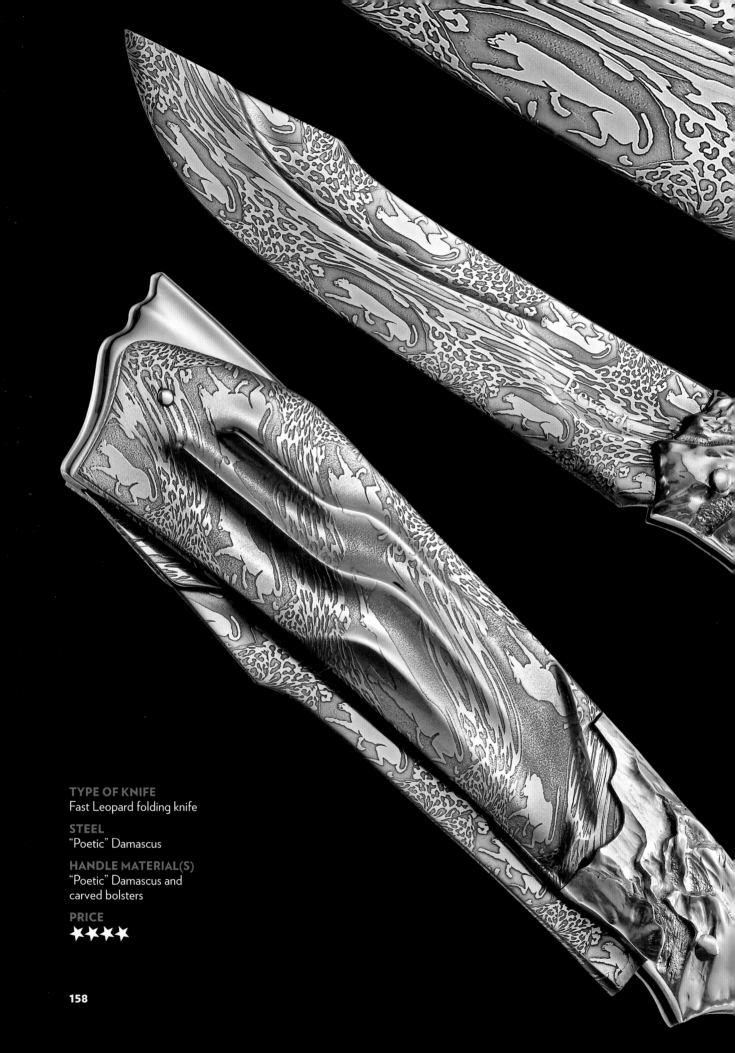

TYPE OF KNIFE
Fast Leopard folding knife

STEEL
"Poetic" Damascus

HANDLE MATERIAL(S)
"Poetic" Damascus and
carved bolsters

PRICE
★★★★

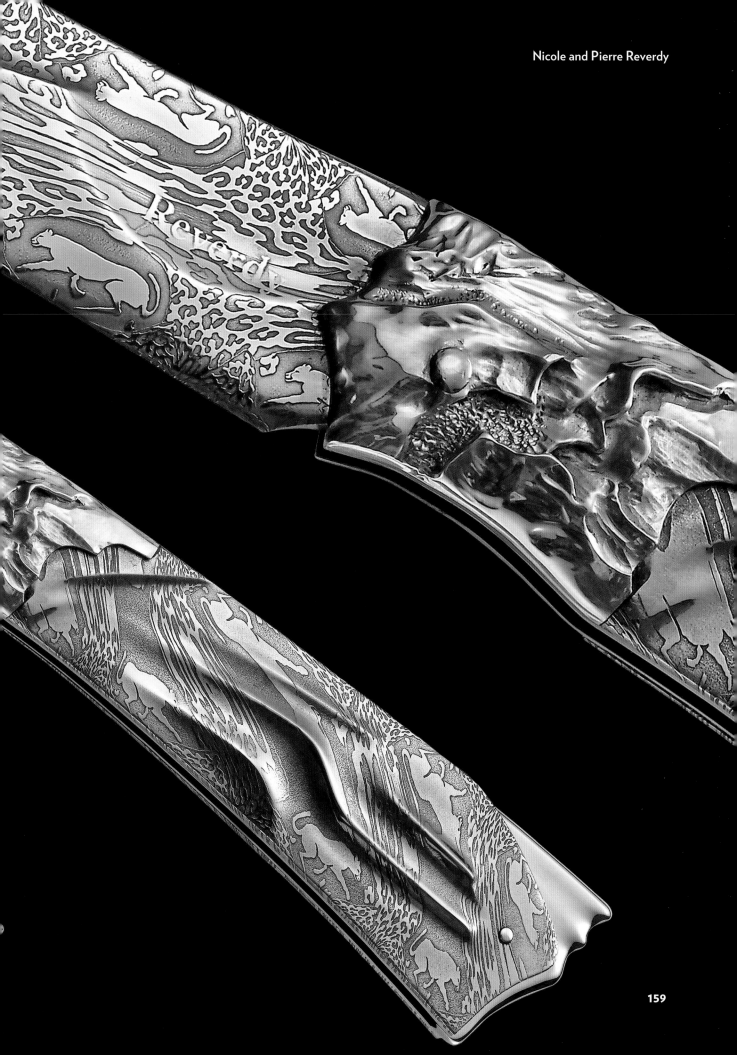

CHARLES ROULIN

Charles Roulin discovered fine art knifemaking later on in life (at 48), by pure chance. Among many professions, he has been a photographer, an art restorer, and has made fly rods for anglers. Incidentally, one of his clients was a prominent Swiss collector who introduced him to the world of fine art knifemaking. This collector helped him undertake a course with a couple of sculptors and knifemakers, Jody and Butch Beaver, in Arizona. Very skilled with his hands, Charles Roulin decided to make his first knives, which he also carved. At 52, he became a fine art knifemaker.

He designs pieces that leave large areas to carve. Little by little, his technique evolved, and he acquired high performance equipment and quickly became a key figure in the world of high-end knifemaking. Some of his pieces are carved completely in 3D, they are often remarkable wildlife scenes or "impressionist" paintings.

Each knife represents hours spent behind huge fiber optic binoculars. The subjects are worked in the most modern and high-quality materials, as well as Damascus steel made by the best blacksmiths. Nothing is welded or attached; everything is carved entirely from the same piece of material.

Charles Roulin works his subjects in such a way that they appear frozen in motion, almost like a snapshot. That's why each new piece is a new adventure, long and sometimes challenging: one false movement, one jolt and it would be disaster, which often can't be repaired.

Making a 3D knife can take one week to several months of work. Therefore, each of his knives is a unique piece.

Charles Roulin does not participate in many exhibitions (FICX-Paris, Milan).

www.coutelier-roulin.art

TYPE OF KNIFE
Letter opener

STEEL
Stainless Damascus integral

HANDLE MATERIAL(S)
Entirely carved knife
(hunting scenes from
the time of Neanderthal
man with mammoths and
wolves).

PRICE

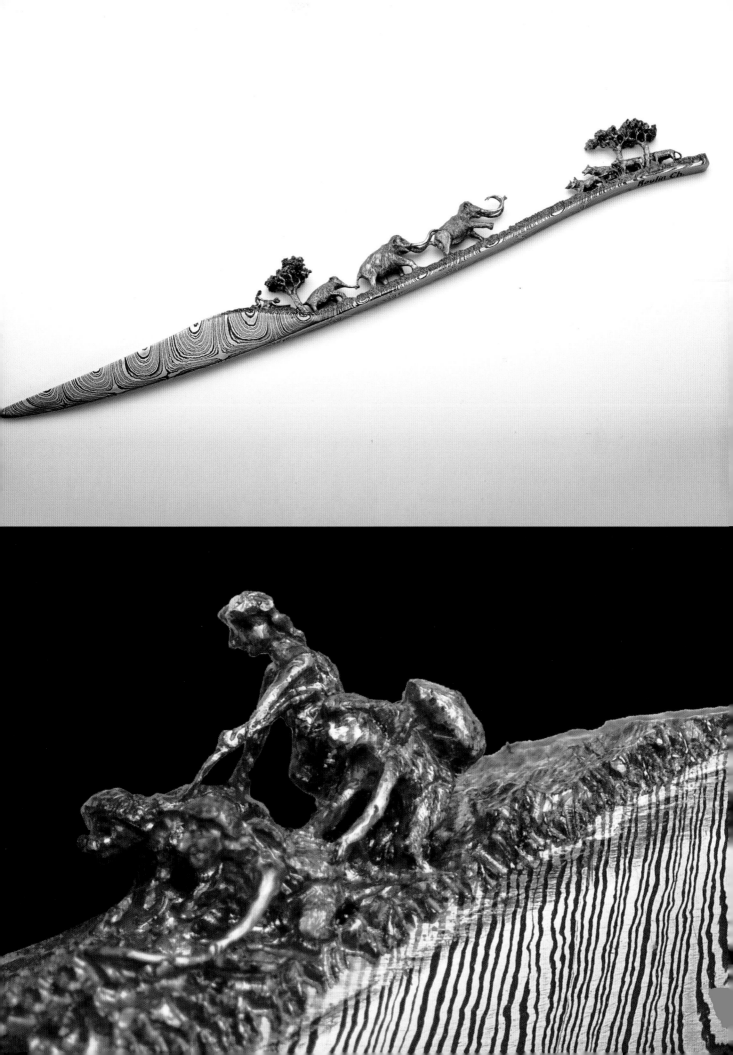

TYPE OF KNIFE
3D Lizard folding knife

LOCKING SYSTEM (FOR FOLDING KNIVES)
Slipjoint

STEEL
Twisted Damascus

HANDLE MATERIAL(S)
Carved steel and stabilized birch

PRICE
★★★

TYPE OF KNIFE
Nine Dragons folding knife

LOCKING SYSTEM (FOR FOLDING KNIVES)
Slipjoint

STEEL
440C carved

HANDLE MATERIAL(S)
Fully carved titanium
(Asian-themed)

PRICE

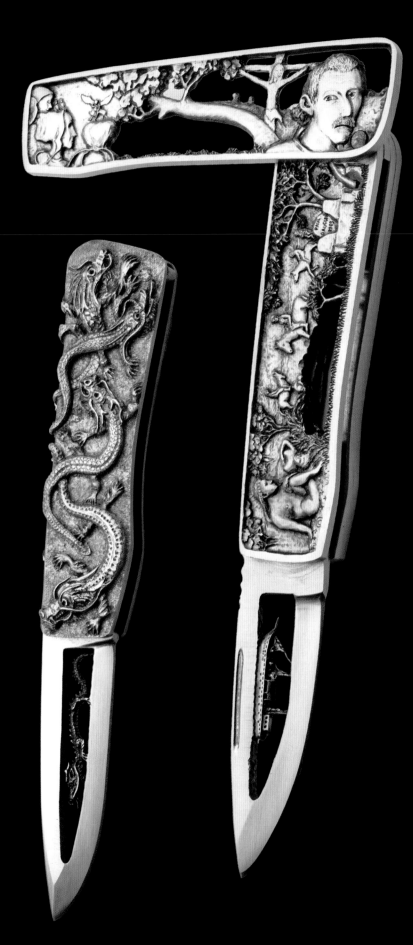

KYLE ROYER

Kyle Royer is a sensation: born in 1990, he became a Journeyman Smith at the age of 18 and Master Smith at 20, which made him the second youngest MS after Josh Smith.

When he was a child, his front door was the school gate, and his schoolyard went as far as the eye could see! This is because Mr. and Mrs. Royer were fans of homeschooling. At the age of 12, Kyle never left the house without his machete attached to his belt... except to the town center. When he turned 16, his mother decided that it was time for him to spread his wings. By chance, she read an article in the local paper about a famous knifemaker who lived nearby: Don Hanson. She talked to Kyle about it, who responded: "Make a knife? Why not?" Thanks to his childhood experiences, his first knife was made in the style of those worn on the belts of local hunters: with a white-tailed deer antler handle. Kyle was very proud of this first tool, which his father was quick to share with the whole family and the neighborhood. It was time to move on to the next step, and it wasn't a small one: the Bill Moran School of Bladesmithing, at Texarkana College (Texas). "When I was 16, for the first time in my life, I went to school!" he explained. Kyle Royer is a young American in his prime, who lives a healthy life, far from the hustle and bustle of big cities.

Kyle produces gorgeous Bowie knives, daggers and hunting knives, most often in multi-bar Damascus steel. He is one of the most talented blacksmiths of his generation, and his work is beautifully photographed by his brother Caleb.

Every year, he participates in the BLADE Show Atlanta and the AKA Custom Knife Show in Little Rock, Arkansas.

www.kyleroyerknives.com

TYPE OF KNIFE
Recurve Bowie
Double Edge

STEEL
Mosaic Damascus
(1084/15N20)

HANDLE MATERIAL(S)
Fossilized walrus tooth.
Blued steel guard and
pommel with inlaid gold
threads

PRICE
★★★★

TYPE OF KNIFE
Bowie

STEEL
Mosaic Damascus

HANDLE MATERIAL(S)
Scales made from pearl
oyster mother-of-pearl.
Guard made from
"clamshell" Damascus
steel, pommel made from
Damascus steel with gold
thread. Sheath made of
leather and exotic skins by
the artist

SIZE
266 mm (total)
150 mm (blade)

PRICE
★★★★

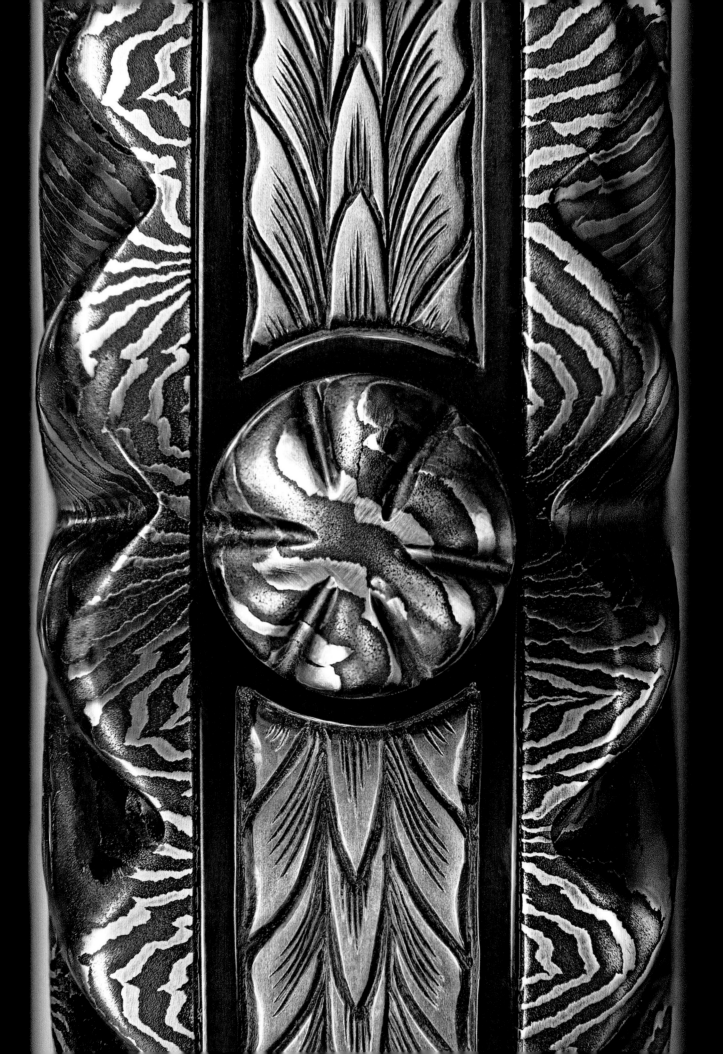

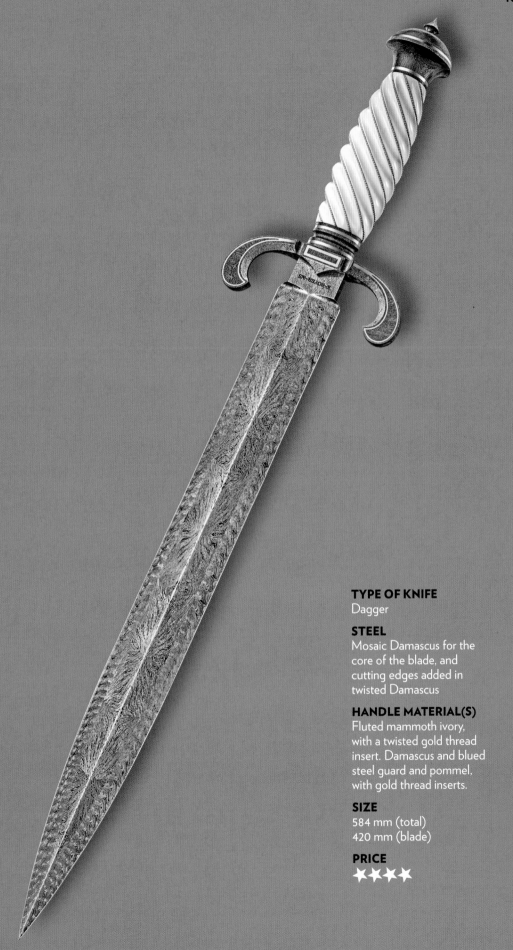

TYPE OF KNIFE
Dagger

STEEL
Mosaic Damascus for the
core of the blade, and
cutting edges added in
twisted Damascus

HANDLE MATERIAL(S)
Fluted mammoth ivory,
with a twisted gold thread
insert. Damascus and blued
steel guard and pommel,
with gold thread inserts.

SIZE
584 mm (total)
420 mm (blade)

PRICE
★★★★

STEVEN SCHWARZER

A young knifemaker at barely 71, Steven Schwarzer has been forging since 1972! He made his first Damascus knives in 1976, at a time when the style was not as popular as it is now. There were no Internet tutorials or forums, and very few books. It was the good old days, when anything could still be invented... and Steven was one of those who invented many new things in this field. He didn't forget to pay a moving tribute to the person who brought Damascus steel to America: William F. Moran Jr, co-founder of the American Bladesmith Society (with Bill Bagwell, Don Hastings, and B.R. Hughes) in 1972. Steven Schwarzer has been a Mastersmith with the ABS since 1983. As an inventor of many new techniques, he contributed greatly to the creation of mosaic Damascus and patterned Damascus. Something that he enjoys, even now, is teaching others about his art in master classes at his workshop in Florida or at forging symposiums. An experienced blacksmith and knifemaker, he has experience in all aspects of knifemaking, from rustic primitive American knives to the most luxurious folding knives with sophisticated locking systems. He's also had an impact on the knifemaking industry as a whole.

His wife, Lora, is also a knifemaker and blacksmith.

Many of his students have become famous and respected knifemakers.

Steven Schwarzer continues to be a very active knifemaker and mentor, showing his work at BLADE Show Atlanta each year. He also works with *BLADE Magazine*.

www.steveschwarzer.com

TYPE OF KNIFE
The Hunter folding knife

LOCKING SYSTEM (FOR FOLDING KNIVES)
Slipjoint

STEEL
Mosaic Damascus body (which made this knifemaker famous throughout the knifemaking world)

HANDLE MATERIAL(S)
Damascus steel bolster and mammoth ivory scales

SIZE
190 mm (open)

PRICE
★★

TYPE OF KNIFE
Folding knife

LOCKING SYSTEM (FOR FOLDING KNIVES)
Liner lock, with "one-handed" opening

STEEL
Heat-colored mosaic Damascus, mother-of-pearl button (thumb stud)

HANDLE MATERIAL(S)
Heat-colored mosaic Damascus with mammoth ivory scales

PRICE
★★★

TYPE OF KNIFE
New Persian folding knife

LOCKING SYSTEM (FOR FOLDING KNIVES)
Liner lock with button opening integrated into the bolster

STEEL
Mosaic Palm Leaf Damascus

HANDLE MATERIAL(S)
Palm leaf mosaic Damascus and fossilized walrus tooth

SIZE
235 mm (open)

PRICE
★★

TYPE OF KNIFE
Folding knife, with
automatic opening

**LOCKING SYSTEM (FOR
FOLDING KNIVES)**
Liner lock

STEEL
Chevron Damascus

HANDLE MATERIAL(S)
Heat-colored "Virus"
Mosaic Damascus bolsters,
mother-of-pearl scales

SIZE
222 mm (open)
101 mm (blade)

PRICE
★★★

KEN STEIGERWALT

In 1978, when Ken was just 15, he made his first knife, at the kitchen table, with just a few filing tools. As his ideas continued to form, others came to mind as well. Just three years later, he became a full-time knifemaker! Suffice to say that Ken Steigerwalt was a very promising knife maker. Since then, he has endeavored to ensure each of his creations is more accomplished than the last.

And he didn't start small. From the moment he started making knives, he has been making folding knives with mid-lock systems, which are far from the easiest.

Since then, he has experimented with many locking systems, and has even invented some.

A Steigerwalt knife is not an everyday piece. Often inspired by the Art Deco or Bauhaus styles, with geometric shapes, its design may appear to be simple, as is often the case with perfect pieces.

Ken Steigerwalt has also received eleven awards in just seven appearances at BLADE Show, the big event in Atlanta (he has not been in the competition since 2008). He uses the rarest available materials, such as meteorite, antique tortoise shell, or a mosaic of his own making, in which he incorporates mother-of-pearl, gold and stones into Bakelite.

He lives in Orangeville, Pennsylvania, and participates in shows in Solvang (California), Milan, the BLADE Show and FICX-Paris.

www.steigerwaltknives.com

"I like to look at reproductions of works of art. Often, a detail catches my eye and becomes a source of inspiration in my creative process. I don't do a lot of sketches to figure out the design of my knives. I usually have a picture in my mind and a clear idea of what they will look like."

TYPE OF KNIFE
Bauhaus folding knife
Max Wedge

LOCKING SYSTEM (FOR FOLDING KNIVES)
Back lock

STEEL
CPM-154

HANDLE MATERIAL(S)
416 stainless steel with gold, meteorite and black shell inserts

PRICE
★★★

TYPE OF KNIFE
Helix folding knife

LOCKING SYSTEM (FOR FOLDING KNIVES)
Back lock

STEEL
CPM-154

HANDLE MATERIAL(S)
416 stainless steel with Bakelite, meteorite, bone, shell and gold inserts

PRICE
★★★★

TYPE OF KNIFE
Bauhaus folding knife

LOCKING SYSTEM (FOR FOLDING KNIVES)
Back lock

STEEL
Damasteel©

HANDLE MATERIAL(S)
416 stainless steel with tortoiseshell (farmed in accordance with CITES) and gold inserts

PRICE
★★★

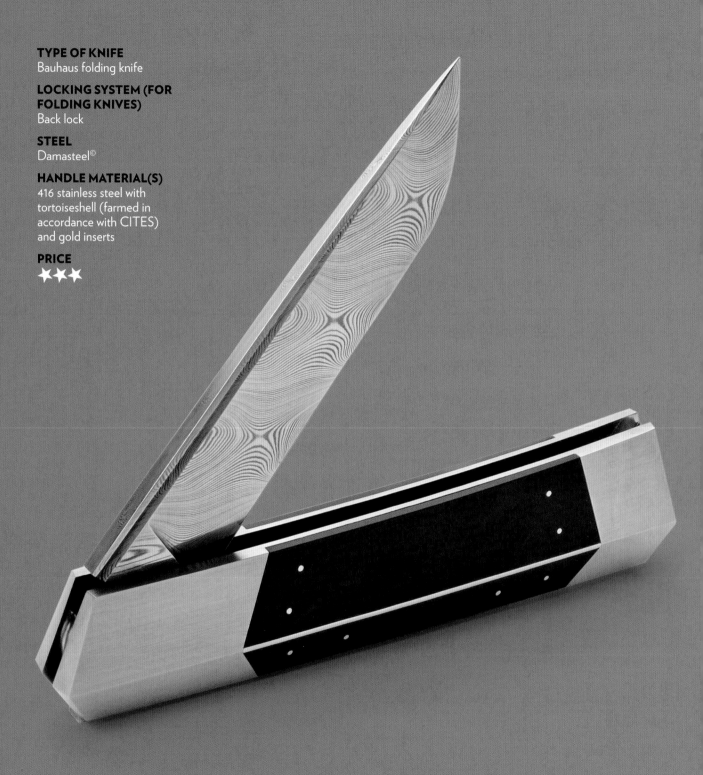

TYPE OF KNIFE
Bauhaus folding knife

LOCKING SYSTEM (FOR FOLDING KNIVES)
Back lock

STEEL
CPM-154 and gold

HANDLE MATERIAL(S)
416 stainless steel with gold, meteorite and shell inserts

PRICE
★★★★

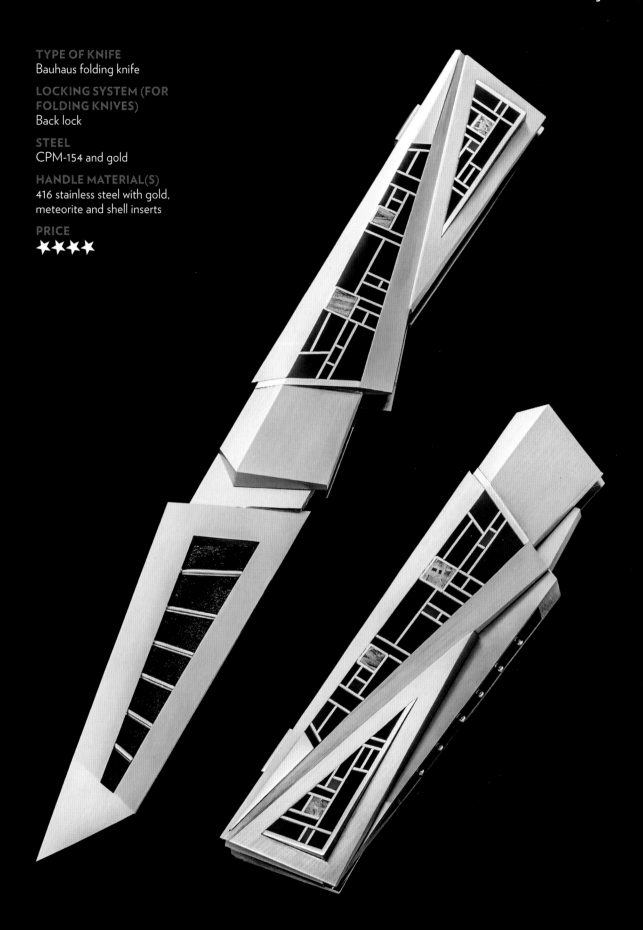

JUERGEN STEINAU

Juergen Steinau was born in 1953 in what was then still East Berlin. At 14, he began studying metalwork. He made all sorts of items, producing his first folding knife in 1982.

In 1989, he was granted an exit visa and participated in the Munich knife-making show. His knives already possessed a very individual, accomplished style.

He then participated in the first SICAC knife show, in Paris, and after the fall of the Berlin Wall (1989) and German reunification, he was able to travel to the United States and attend the New York show in 1991.

After that, everything else fell into place: joining the American Guild, then the Italian Guild, and being included among the 25 knifemakers invited to the AKI in San Diego.

Considering the complexity of his knives, Juergen makes very few: a maximum of one knife per month. For this reason, he does not participate in many shows and usually only has one knife to show (sometimes, it's a knife being delivered to one of his customers).

His knives are made of up to 35 pieces and are assembled with extreme precision. His waiting list is more than five years.

His workshop is located in a quiet neighborhood of what was once East Berlin, in a house that was almost in ruins when he bought it, which he rebuilt himself.

He can be found in this sanctuary every day, where, all year round, he spends his days from 9 o'clock in the morning to 8 o'clock in the evening, with just an hour lunchbreak! Here there are no lasers, no digital machines, only traditionally (and fairly old) German machine tools, with which he is very familiar and can get the best results.

The reunification of West and East Germany did not change much for him. "Okay, now we can now travel abroad more freely."

Jurgen Steinau is an unusual and captivating person.

"Most things that I make can be described as something between art and craft. The term "applied arts" would be appropriate. Some of my pieces are more like tools, others are more like sculptures. Sometimes, the difference is subtle."

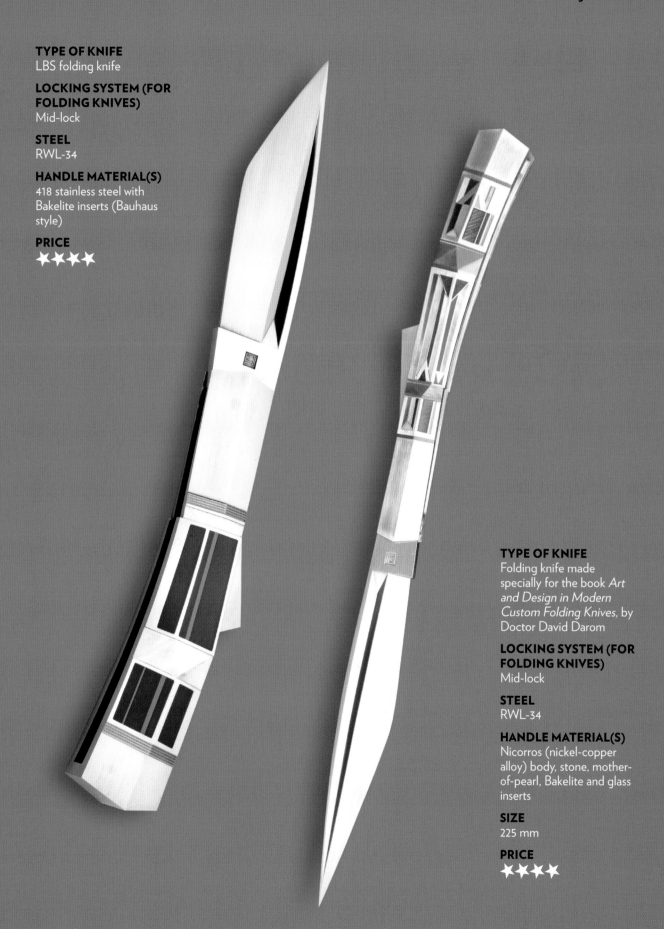

TYPE OF KNIFE
LBS folding knife

LOCKING SYSTEM (FOR FOLDING KNIVES)
Mid-lock

STEEL
RWL-34

HANDLE MATERIAL(S)
418 stainless steel with Bakelite inserts (Bauhaus style)

PRICE
★★★★

TYPE OF KNIFE
Folding knife made specially for the book *Art and Design in Modern Custom Folding Knives*, by Doctor David Darom

LOCKING SYSTEM (FOR FOLDING KNIVES)
Mid-lock

STEEL
RWL-34

HANDLE MATERIAL(S)
Nicorros (nickel-copper alloy) body, stone, mother-of-pearl, Bakelite and glass inserts

SIZE
225 mm

PRICE
★★★★

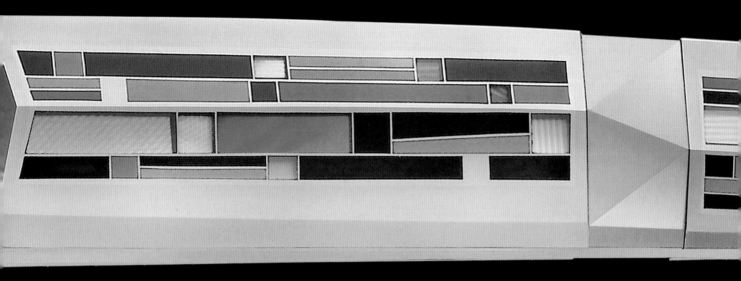

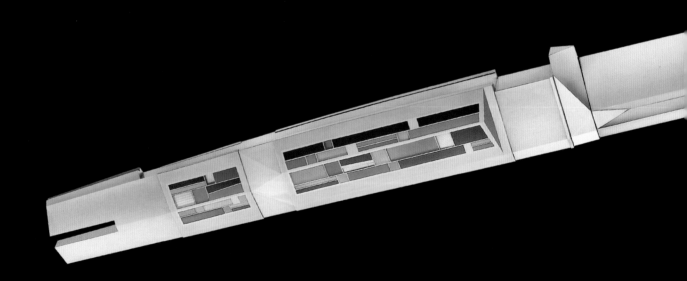

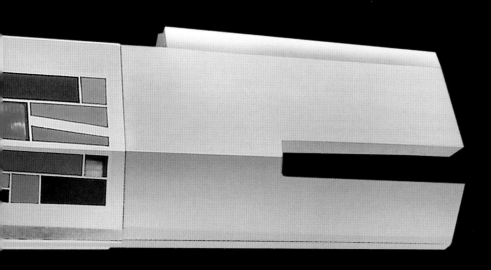

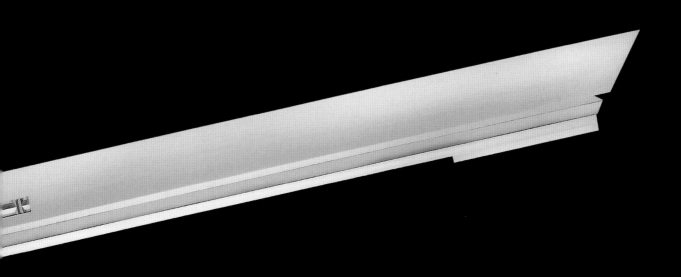

TYPE OF KNIFE
Fix Cutter

STEEL
440B

HANDLE MATERIAL(S)
416 stainless steel and 14
karat gold, with stone and
Bakelite inserts

PRICE

JEAN-PIERRE SUCHERAS

At the age of 14, Jean-Pierre Sucheras started learning about the engineering trades.

He then began his professional life in a small family workshop where he developed the necessary techniques and skills. Jean-Pierre worked for the ministry of defense, as a part-time mechanic-toolmaker in the air force. He dedicated the rest of his time and a lot of his vacation time to knifemaking.

With a rich knowledge base and motivated by his passion for locking systems and small precision engineering, he produced his first knives in the early 1990s. In 1991, equipped with invaluable technical assets and the expert advice of his Canadian friend Denis Lemaire, he made and exhibited his first folding knives with liner lock systems. In 2004, he was the only person to win a *"Un des Meilleurs Ouvriers de France"* (French Craftsperson of the Year) award in the "pocket knife" category. He won the award again in 2007, this time in the "hunting knife" category, along with Jean-Paul Tisseyre and Jean-Michael Cayron.

He is passionate about antique pieces, which he studies in great detail by restoring them, to discover the systems and mechanisms that ancient knife-makers used. He is one of the most frequent visitors to the *Musée de la Coutellerie* (Cutlery Museum) in Thiers, where he is constantly discovering classical techniques.

He likes to work with all styles, from historical to high-tech knives. Generally, his knives are unique pieces, except for a few rare collaborations with industrial knifemaking manufacturers to provide affordable products for everyone.

He has participated in the New York and Boston shows, and he frequently attends the Coutellia, FICX-Paris and Milan shows.

www.sucheras-coutelier.fr

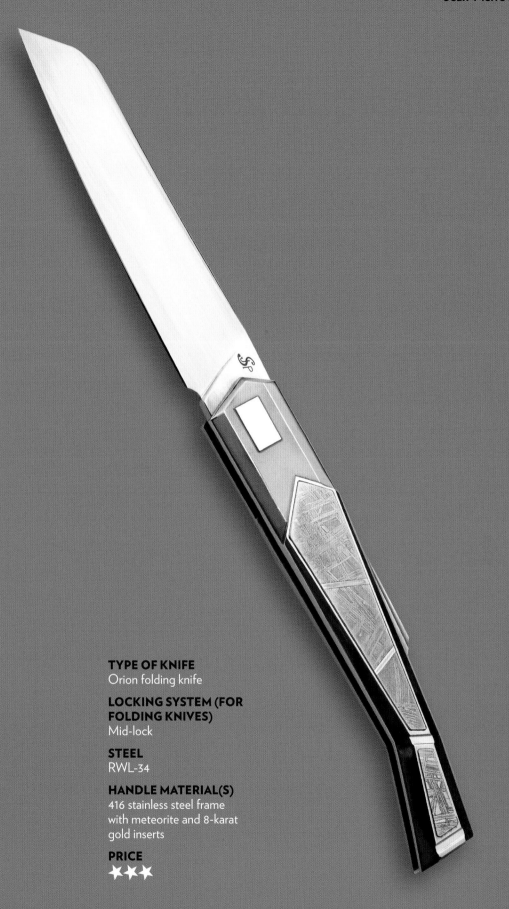

Jean-Pierre Sucheras

TYPE OF KNIFE
Orion folding knife

LOCKING SYSTEM (FOR FOLDING KNIVES)
Mid-lock

STEEL
RWL-34

HANDLE MATERIAL(S)
416 stainless steel frame with meteorite and 8-karat gold inserts

PRICE
★★★

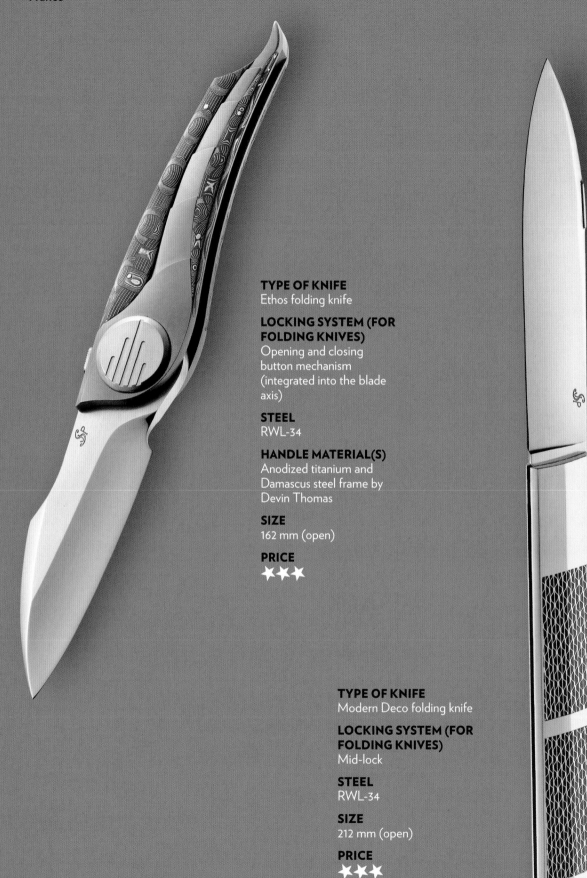

TYPE OF KNIFE
Ethos folding knife

LOCKING SYSTEM (FOR FOLDING KNIVES)
Opening and closing button mechanism (integrated into the blade axis)

STEEL
RWL-34

HANDLE MATERIAL(S)
Anodized titanium and Damascus steel frame by Devin Thomas

SIZE
162 mm (open)

PRICE
★★★

TYPE OF KNIFE
Modern Deco folding knife

LOCKING SYSTEM (FOR FOLDING KNIVES)
Mid-lock

STEEL
RWL-34

SIZE
212 mm (open)

PRICE
★★★

TYPE OF KNIFE
Bouledogue revisité
(Bulldog Revisited) folding
knife

LOCKING SYSTEM (FOR FOLDING KNIVES)
Slipjoint

STEEL
RWL-34

HANDLE MATERIAL(S)
Grey anodized titanium
frame and mammoth hide
scales

PRICE
★★

ANDRÉ THORBURN

André Thorburn was born in 1956 in Johannesburg. He grew up on a family farm and learned how to look after himself from a very young age.

He entered the world of knifemaking in the same way as some people enter into religion, in 1989.

He sold his first knife a year later and joined the South African Guild in 1995. In 1996, he became a full-time knifemaker and started spending time with the best knifemakers in the world. In 2006, he was admitted to the famous American Knifemakers Guild and won the award for best new member. Other awards followed, at practically all the exhibitions in which he participated. He specializes in high-end folding knives and uses ultra-modern methods: laser and waterjet cutting, as well as computer-assisted design and fabrication. André particularly likes making high-caliber tactical folding knives, with blades fitted on ball bearings (IKBS). He was Chairman of the South African Guild from 2007 to 2011. In 2007, André and his wife (who collaborates on a lot of his knives) returned to the family farm in Warmbaths (renamed Bela Bela), in the bush, where they lead a peaceful life. André sometimes leaves to attend a few far-away shows: New Jersey (NYCKS), the BLADE Show, and the USN Gathering in Las Vegas (in August).

www.andrethorburn.com

TYPE OF KNIFE
Folding knife

LOCKING SYSTEM (FOR FOLDING KNIVES)
Liner lock

STEEL
RWL-34

HANDLE MATERIAL(S)
Carbon fiber scales with engraved inserts

PRICE

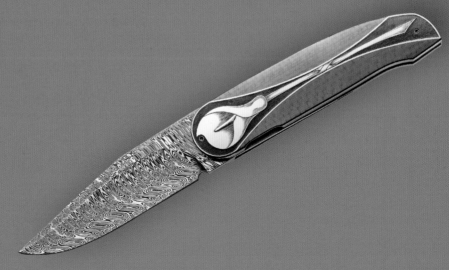

André Thorburn

TYPE OF KNIFE
Folding knife

LOCKING SYSTEM (FOR FOLDING KNIVES)
Liner lock flipper (IKBS ceramic bearing)

STEEL
Takefu san mai SG2

HANDLE MATERIAL(S)
Carbon fiber with Arizona desert ironwood inserts. Titanium clip.

SIZE
210 mm (open)

PRICE
★★★

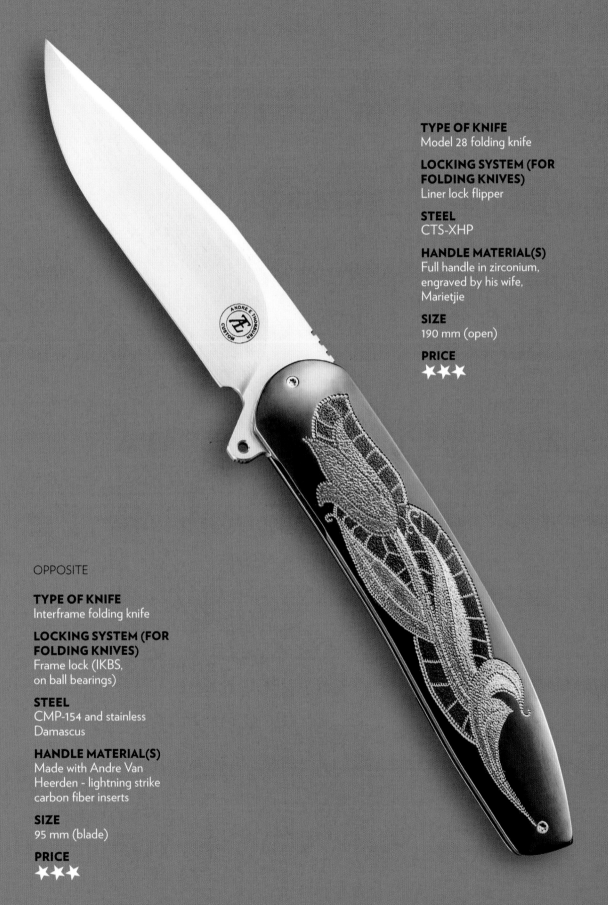

TYPE OF KNIFE
Model 28 folding knife

LOCKING SYSTEM (FOR FOLDING KNIVES)
Liner lock flipper

STEEL
CTS-XHP

HANDLE MATERIAL(S)
Full handle in zirconium, engraved by his wife, Marietjie

SIZE
190 mm (open)

PRICE
★★★

OPPOSITE

TYPE OF KNIFE
Interframe folding knife

LOCKING SYSTEM (FOR FOLDING KNIVES)
Frame lock (IKBS, on ball bearings)

STEEL
CMP-154 and stainless Damascus

HANDLE MATERIAL(S)
Made with Andre Van Heerden - lightning strike carbon fiber inserts

SIZE
95 mm (blade)

PRICE
★★★

PEKKA TUOMINEN

Pekka Tuominen has worked in a few very different fields, first as a teacher, a farmer, and then as a soldier in the Middle East and the Balkans.

When he was younger, he was a Boy Scout, and then he trained to be a desert guide. He has always liked the great outdoors and always carries a knife with him. It was only one step from that point to making knives, a step he happily took in 2007! He became a blacksmith and then a mastersmith.

In the beginning, the path was clear. In Finland, where there is a strong knifemaking tradition, he made puukkos, whose simple lines he appreciated.

During his first shows abroad, he discovered a different type of knifemaking that would have an influence on him. His style developed towards more modern knifemaking (both with regards to shapes and the materials used), whilst maintaining a distinctly Nordic style: a new style of Nordic knifemaking was born! The lines of his knives, both fixed-blade and folding, are simple and almost meticulous. Nothing is decided on a whim. The knives are out of this world! Today, Pekka Tuominen has earned an international reputation.

In 2019, he participated in the Helsinki, Las Vegas and FICX-Paris shows.

www.puukkopekka.com

TYPE OF KNIFE
Faces fixed blade

STEEL
San mai composite

HANDLE MATERIAL(S)
Fossilized walrus tooth

PRICE
★★

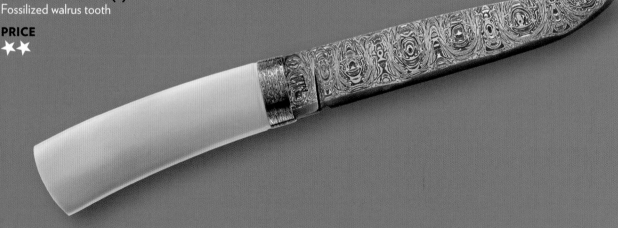

TYPE OF KNIFE
Nordic-style fixed blade

STEEL
Damascus

HANDLE MATERIAL(S)
Fossilized walrus ivory

SIZE
130 mm

PRICE
★ ★

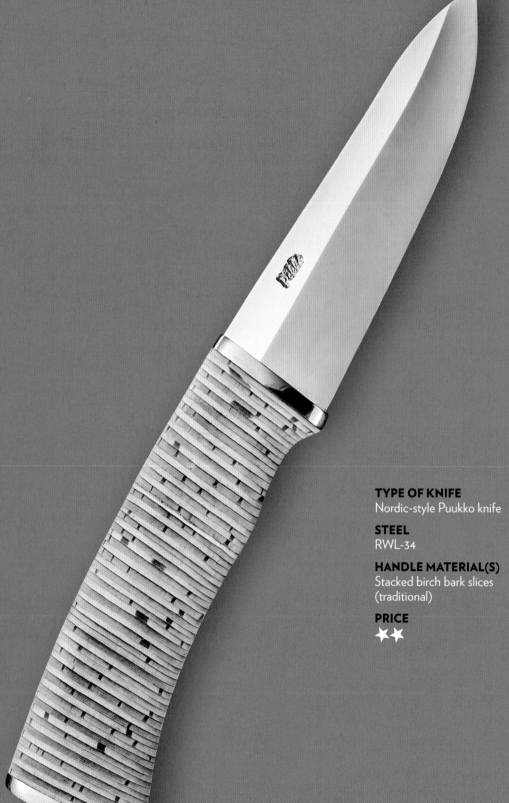

TYPE OF KNIFE
Nordic-style Puukko knife

STEEL
RWL-34

HANDLE MATERIAL(S)
Stacked birch bark slices
(traditional)

PRICE
★★

TYPE OF KNIFE
Push dagger

STEEL
Damascus (15N20/1080)

HANDLE MATERIAL(S)
Fossilized walrus ivory

SIZE
130 mm

PRICE
★★

ALAIN VALETTE

Alain Valette was born in 1962, just above the family forge. He took over the business in 1987: agricultural mechanics and small tools were on the menu.

He made his first knife in 1986, on a bet, and got a taste for it - so much so that he registered as an amateur in the first *Salon International du Couteau d'Art et de Collection* (Paris Knife Show, SICAC) in 1990. Since then, he has continued to create avant-garde models with complex mechanisms, which he spends hours perfecting. You could say that he's a "perfectionist", which wouldn't bother him! But behind his light-hearted character, there is a part of him that is constantly looking to progress. He's blessed with a great imagination, which can lead him into projects where even he doesn't always know what he's doing! For example, his "Talisman de Poséidon" (Poseidon's Talisman), "Rêve de Chronos" (Chronos' Dream) or "Art-Chimède" (Art-chimedes).

He's a specialist in the retro-futuristic, *steampunk*, "why do something easy when you can do something complicated", gearworks style. He is a master of gears and cogs. Fine watchmaking inspires him a great deal. Alain Valette enjoys creating unusual knives that tell a story. He has projects lined up for the next one hundred years, including learning how to do 3D engraving.

He participates in FICX-Paris, as well as the Agde show.

www.couteauxvalette.com

TYPE OF KNIFE
Volcano Sunset, a figurative folding knife that represents a volcano with flowing lava

LOCKING SYSTEM (FOR FOLDING KNIVES)
Opens and closes with a button (representing the sun)

STEEL
Carved Damascus

HANDLE MATERIAL(S)
Amboyna burl

PRICE

★★★

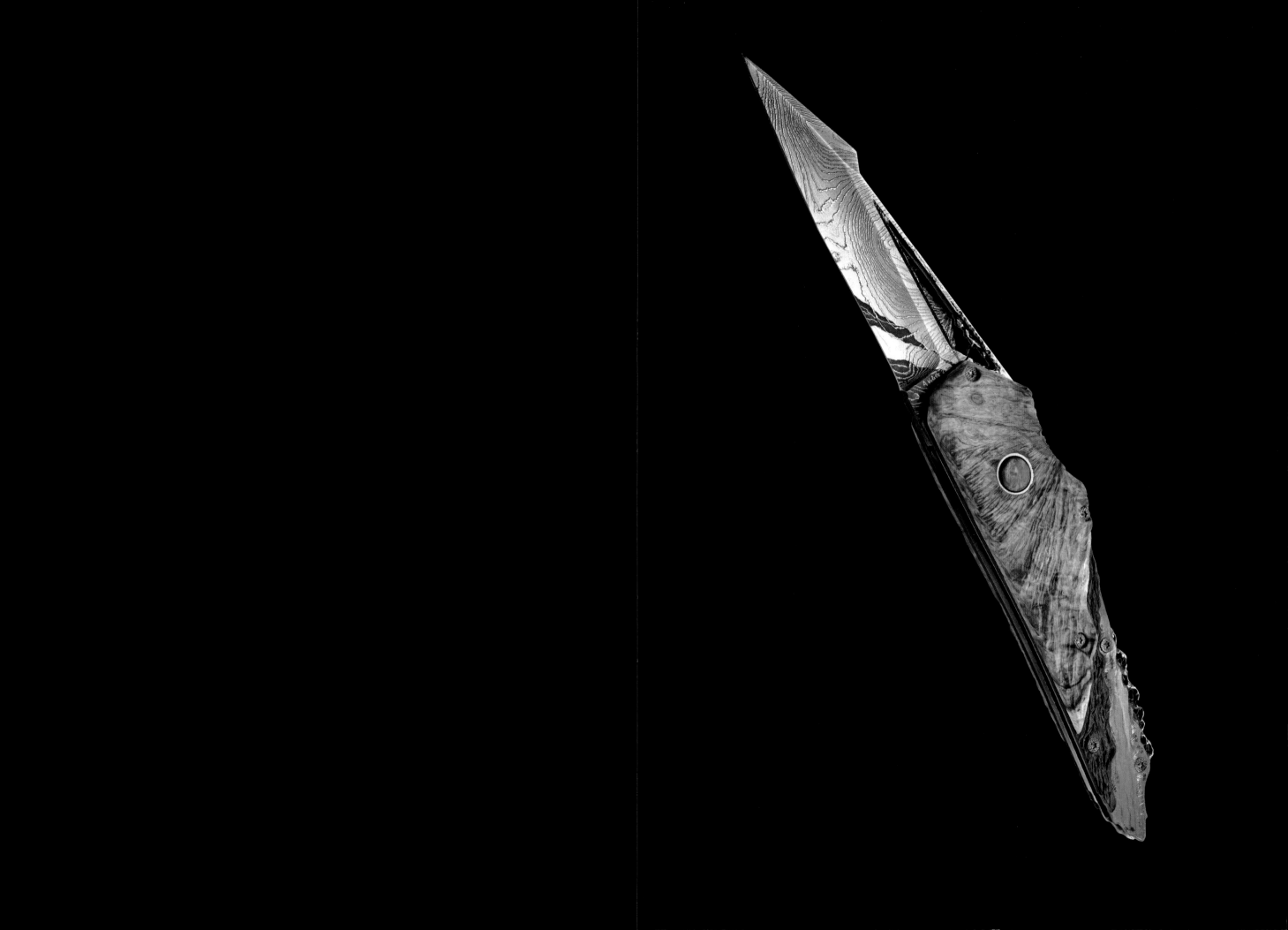

TYPE OF KNIFE
Project X folding knife

LOCKING SYSTEM (FOR FOLDING KNIVES)
Opening controlled by extractable push button, with double mechanical system resulting in a "daring" scene... hidden in a trap door

STEEL
Twisted Damascus

HANDLE MATERIAL(S)
Titanium, epoxy and brass

PRICE
★★★★

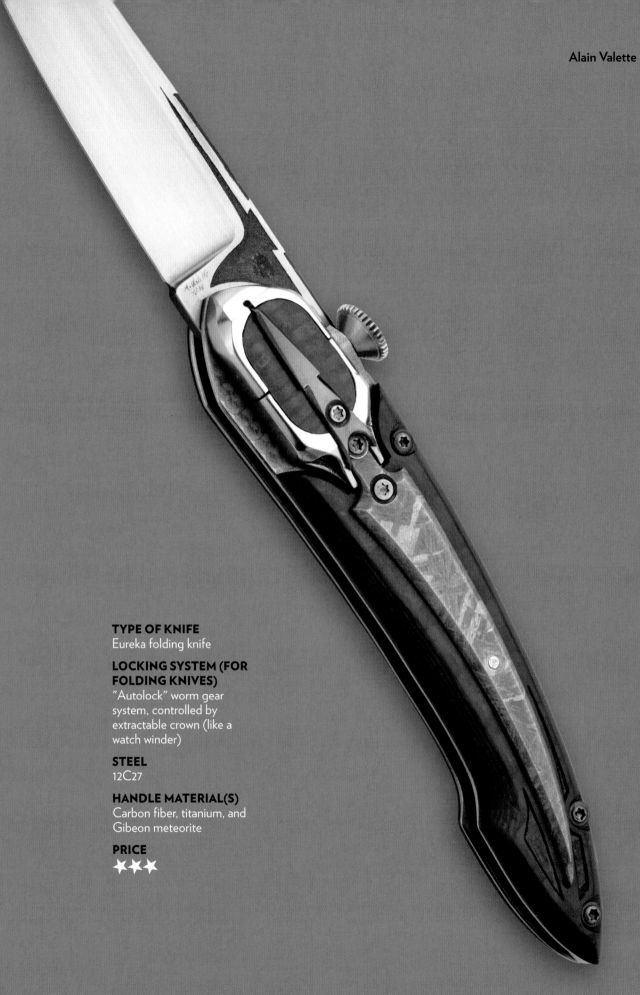

Alain Valette

TYPE OF KNIFE
Eureka folding knife

LOCKING SYSTEM (FOR FOLDING KNIVES)
"Autolock" worm gear system, controlled by extractable crown (like a watch winder)

STEEL
12C27

HANDLE MATERIAL(S)
Carbon fiber, titanium, and Gibeon meteorite

PRICE
★★★

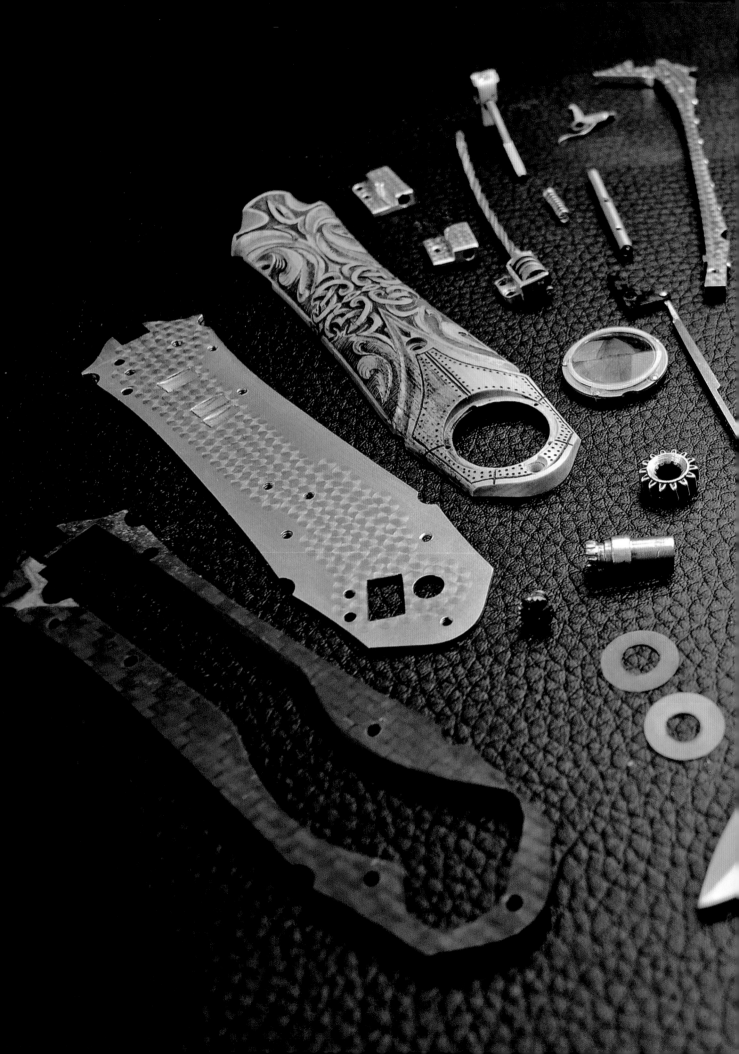

HENRI VIALLON

A child of Thiers, Henri Viallon is a mechanic-toolmaker by training.

In 1983, at 25, he joined the *Maison des Couteliers* (Cutlery Museum) as head of production. He is passionate about the collections in the *Musée de la Coutellerie* (Cutlery Museum); it brings together collectors, specialists and professionals and promotes production in Thiers.

He is extremely interested in forging, and was one of the first French knifemakers to take an interest in Damascus steel, rediscovered by William Moran on the other side of the Atlantic. Feeling creative, he turned towards fine art knives, still in its infancy in France, and established his own business in 1987. For Henri, knowledge is meant to be shared. This is evidenced by his continuous presence in the professional world, both in terms of organizing courses (many reputable French knifemakers have been trained by him), and his collaborations with businesses for certain high-quality industrial fabrications. The complete list of his designs is long: the Sauveterre, the Couteau du Raid Gauloise, the Laguiole +, the Coustel pour Jean-Pierre Coffe.

In 1991, he was given the *"Un des Meilleurs Ouvriers de France"* (French Craftsperson of the Year) award, and in 1994, the Minister of Culture asked him to become one of the 40 artisans sitting on the *Conseil des Métiers d'Art* (Art Trade Council). He made a set of twenty regional knives for the *Musée de la Coutellerie* (Cutlery Museum) in Thiers, each with a different type of Damascus steel blade (he has a second set in his private collection). In 2000, he received the *Premier Prix National des Métiers d'Art* (First National Trade Arts Award, from SEMA), in which 22 candidates were competing from all over France. He went on to collaborate with various Michelin-star chefs to create, among other things, an oyster knife, the "Cancalais", for Olivier Roellinger, a Laguiole with Michel Bras and a Thiers for Joël Robuchon's workshops.

Henri Viallon is no longer making knives.

Henri Viallon

TYPE OF KNIFE
Les Planètes folding knife

LOCKING SYSTEM (FOR FOLDING KNIVES)
Slipjoint

STEEL
Twisted and mosaic Damascus

HANDLE MATERIAL(S)
"Carbon" steel inlaid with mosaic Damascus inserts

SIZE
60 mm (open)

PRICE

TYPE OF KNIFE
Sgian Dubh fixed blade (traditional Scottish knife)

STEEL
Twisted two-bar Damascus

HANDLE MATERIAL(S)
Ebony (carving by Serge Raoux)

PRICE

TYPE OF KNIFE
Kard fixed blade (Oriental-inspired)

STEEL
Mosaic and twisted Damascus, with patterns on the body (Paix, Shalom, Peace, Salam)

HANDLE MATERIAL(S)
Antique ivory carved by Serge Raoux. Mosaic Damascus.

PRICE
★★★

TYPE OF KNIFE
Seurre folding knife

LOCKING SYSTEM (FOR FOLDING KNIVES)
Slipjoint

STEEL
Multi-bar Damascus "Liberté, Égalité, Fraternité" (Liberty, Equality, Fraternity) and a sharp edge

HANDLE MATERIAL(S)
The entire handle is made from antique ivory

PRICE
★★

MICHAEL WALKER

Born in 1949, Michael Walker was a jeweler first before receiving a Gerbier knife and a copy of *BLADE Magazine* as a gift. He then began his career as the "pope" of knifemaking, no less!

Where would modern knifemaking be without him? Michael Walker is a great man: he produces the most innovative knives, the most ingenious locking systems, has the highest prices. With more than twenty locking systems invented, including the famous Walker liner lock, with a patent filed in 1980.

With his wife Patricia, who adds wonderful engravings, they enhanced titanium and gave it its well-deserved reputation.

Michael Walker has contributed so much to the knifemaking industry and it can certainly be said that he is one of the people who brought the pocket knife into the modern era. He can also be thanked for the creation of composite "zipper" blades (two materials assembled like a zipper).

Today, a bit of Michael Walker's genius can be found in many folding knives, both hand made or mass-produced. Some of these knives have reached great heights, in all respects. He has mixed stainless Damascus steel, precious metals, meteorite, anodized titanium and complex mechanisms. Michael Walker has lived in Taos, New Mexico, for more than 30 years. He goes to very few shows, in the United States and Europe, sometimes with a knife to sell.

www.artifexgallery.com/michaelknives.html

TYPE OF KNIFE
Folding knife

LOCKING SYSTEM (FOR FOLDING KNIVES)
Walker liner lock

STEEL
Titanium and 154CM zipper-style assembly

HANDLE MATERIAL(S)
Anodized titanium

PRICE
★★★★

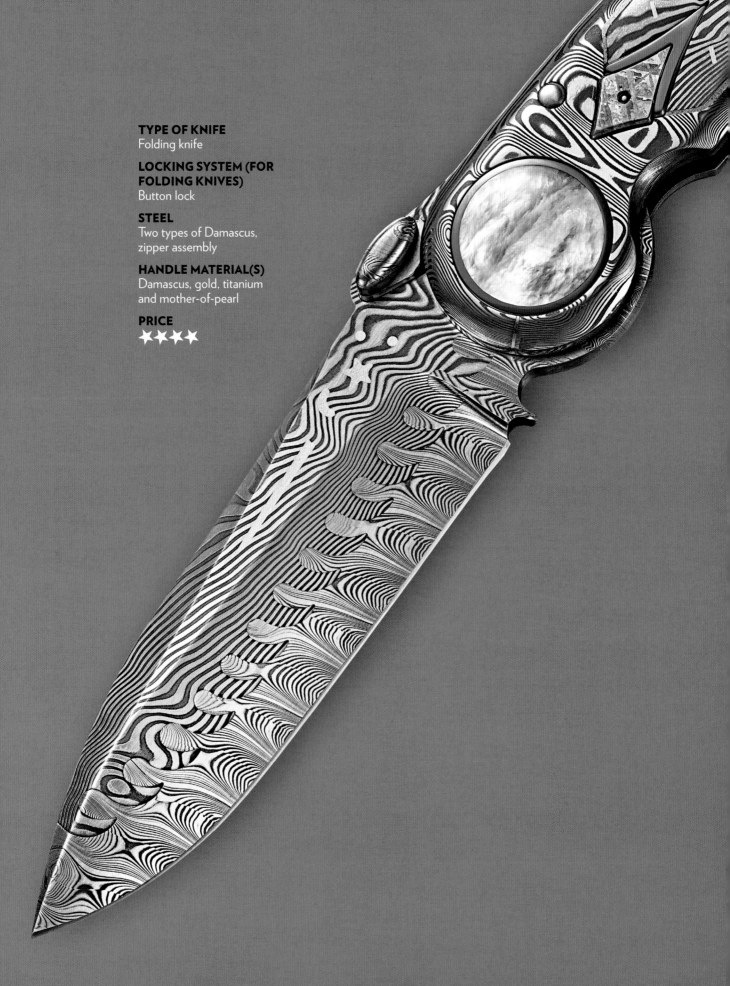

TYPE OF KNIFE
Folding knife

LOCKING SYSTEM (FOR FOLDING KNIVES)
Button lock

STEEL
Two types of Damascus, zipper assembly

HANDLE MATERIAL(S)
Damascus, gold, titanium and mother-of-pearl

PRICE
★★★★

203

TYPE OF KNIFE
Folding knife

LOCKING SYSTEM (FOR FOLDING KNIVES)
Button lock

STEEL
154CM

HANDLE MATERIAL(S)
Anodized and engraved titanium by Patricia Walker

PRICE
★★★★

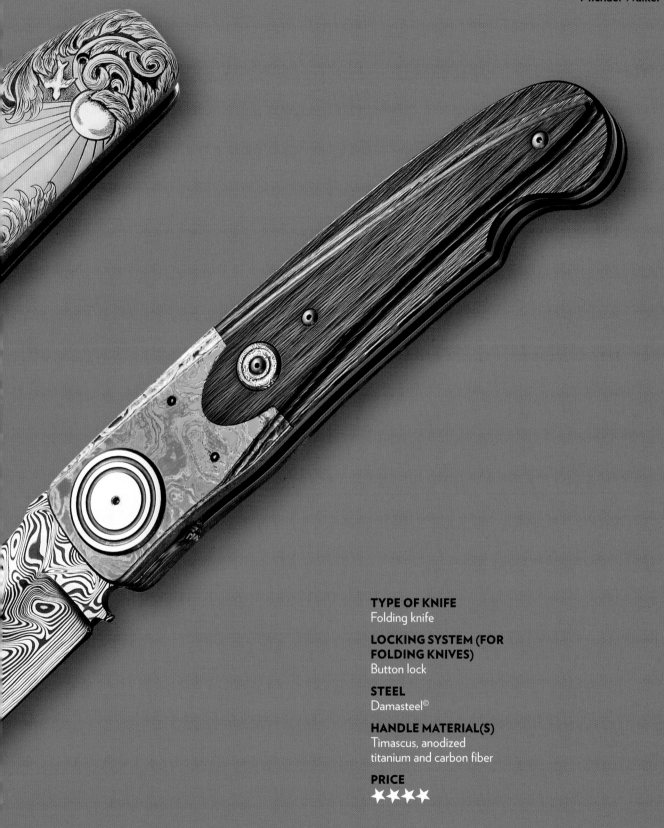

TYPE OF KNIFE
Folding knife

LOCKING SYSTEM (FOR FOLDING KNIVES)
Button lock

STEEL
Damasteel©

HANDLE MATERIAL(S)
Timascus, anodized titanium and carbon fiber

PRICE
★★★★

GLENN WATERS

Glenn did not become a knifemaker until later on in life and was first a jeweler, a trade he still occasionally practices today. Ever since he was young, his biggest passion has been Jujutsu. His father was one of the greatest experts in this field in Australia. He was also introduced to battōdō (the art of cutting with a katana sword). He has visited Japan many times in order to perfect these two disciplines. It is there that he met Masayo, who would become his wife. She is from Hirosaki, a historic city located in the North of Japan's largest island (Honshu), where the couple finally settled down. Glenn has now reached 7th dan (rank) in jujutsu and 3rd dan in battōdō.

He made his first knife in 1993, completely self-taught. And he continued with this, participating in shows, specifically in the Japanese knifemaking capital of Seki, and Matsumoto, then BLADE Show West, in New York, BLADE Show Atlanta, and two shows in Paris. His style often incorporates elements of jewelry, chasing and engraving on his distinctly modern and unique knives. He wins awards at practically all the shows at which he presents his work!

Glenn is not a full-time knifemaker: at first he had an English research chair at Hirosaki university, then he ran his own school, and now he continues to teach part time but is dedicating more and more time to knifemaking. He works at home and particularly likes the long winter days where he lives in Japan as it is one of the snowiest areas. His knives tell a story, often inspired by his adopted country. For this reason, he does not enjoy working on commission. For his blades, he particularly likes Bohler M390 steel and also uses the excellent Japanese steels SGP2 (Super Gold Powder) and VG10 (for the blades he wants to engrave) from Takefu Special Steel, as well as san mai with or without Damascus. For handles, he uses titanium and zirconium, which turns a deep black when heated to red-hot temperatures. He also uses Timascus, with or without coloring, mainly for clips.

www.glennwaters.com

Glenn Waters

TYPE OF KNIFE
Blue Viper 120% folding knife

LOCKING SYSTEM (FOR FOLDING KNIVES)
Frame lock (titanium)

STEEL
Heat-colored "cloudy" Damascus

HANDLE MATERIAL(S)
Anodized titanium

SIZE
195 mm (open)
83 mm (blade)
115 mm (closed)

PRICE
★★★

TYPE OF KNIFE
Shinobi Flipper folding knife

LOCKING SYSTEM (FOR FOLDING KNIVES)
Frame lock (titanium)

STEEL
VG-10 suminagashi san mai

HANDLE MATERIAL(S)
Anodized titanium

SIZE
205 mm (open)
90 mm (blade)
124 mm (closed)

PRICE
★★★

TYPE OF KNIFE
Dragon Tanto fixed blade

STEEL
VG-10 suminagashi san mai. Engravings of Kami (gods of wind and thunder) and two dragons, enhanced with gold

HANDLE MATERIAL(S)
Ray skin and traditional silk lacing

SIZE
280 mm

PRICE
★★★

207

TYPE OF KNIFE
Kaiken folding knife

LOCKING SYSTEM (FOR FOLDING KNIVES)
Liner lock flipper

STEEL
VG-10 suminagashi san mai, gold dragonflies

HANDLE MATERIAL(S)
Titanium, mother-of-pearl, titanium clip with dragonflies added. Maki-e lacquer.

PRICE
★★★

OWEN WOOD

Owen Wood's interest in knifemaking started in 1972, and he soon became the first professional South African knifemaker.

In 1980, he was involved in the creation of a Knifemaker's Guild in his country, of which he remained president for ten years. He participated in his first international exhibition in the United States in 1982, and went on to present his work at shows in Switzerland, France and Germany. In 1999, Owen Wood and his family left South Africa to move to Denver, Colorado. There, Owen collaborated with the brand Spyderco for two years, helping them to set up their factory in Golden. Once his contract had been fulfilled, he became a full-time knifemaker again. For each knife, Owen Wood works from scratch, trying not to be influenced by anything other than his imagination. He doesn't have much of a connection with the knifemaking world. But he does collaborate with some engravers. You could say that his style is similar to that of Art Deco.

Owen Wood participates in the ECCKS in New York and the AKI in San Diego.

TYPE OF KNIFE
Art Deco folding knife

LOCKING SYSTEM (FOR FOLDING KNIVES)
Liner lock

STEEL
Multi-bar Damascus

HANDLE MATERIAL(S)
416 stainless steel with antique tortoiseshell inserts. Art Deco engravings.

PRICE
★★★

TYPE OF KNIFE
Two folding knives

LOCKING SYSTEM (FOR FOLDING KNIVES)
Liner lock

STEEL
Multi-bar Damascus
(fishbone and explosion)

HANDLE MATERIAL(S)
416 stainless steel, mother-of-pearl, engravings by
Amayak Stepanyan

PRICE
★★★

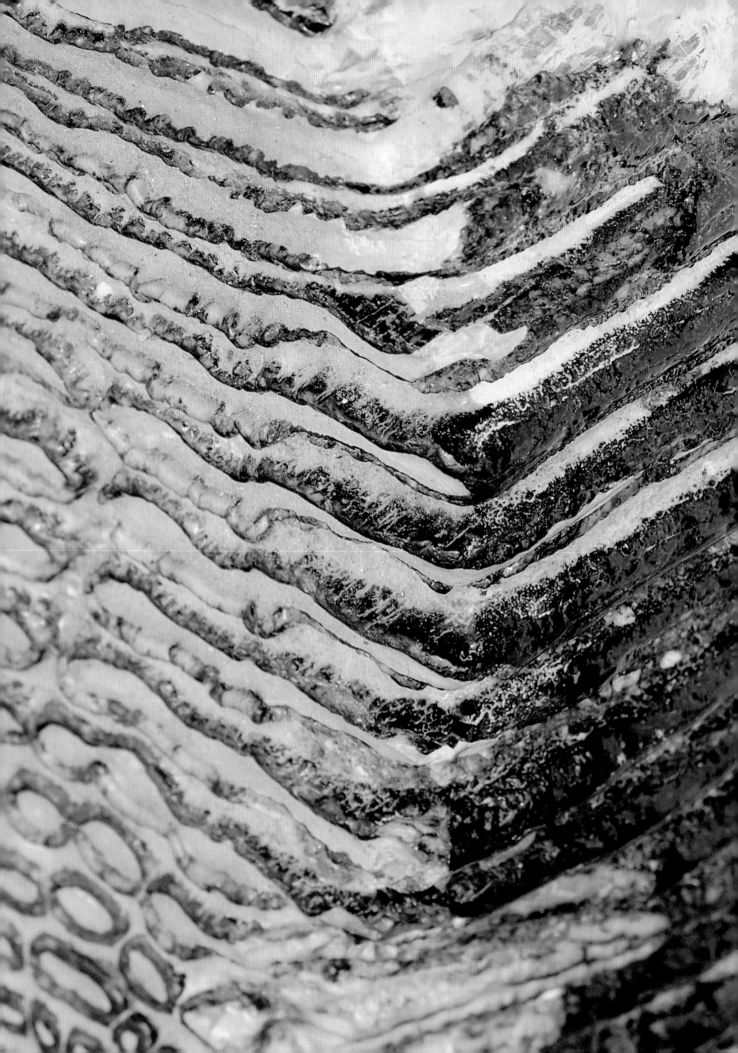

KNIFE HANDLE MATERIALS

UP UNTIL THE START OF THE INDUSTRIAL ERA, MATERIALS FOUND IN NATURE WERE THE ONLY ONES USED TO ADORN KNIFE AND SWORD HANDLES, AND THEY CONTINUE TO BE HIGHLY POPULAR AMONG KNIFEMAKERS AND COLLECTORS.

Today, however, many natural materials of either animal or plant origin are banned under the Washington Convention which regulates their use (in particular, elephant ivory, rhino horn, any part of certain animal species — bones, skin, teeth, or even wood from certain protected tree varieties). Among the most widely used and authorized natural materials, the most popular are certain local or exotic tree varieties, such as Arizona desert ironwood, flame maple, koa, bocote, royal ebony, snakewood, etc. Other products that are widely used include deer antlers, cattle and sheep horns, and horns from other wildlife. Lastly, there is natural, stained or carved bone (to imitate deer antlers). It is also worth giving a special mention to walrus baculum (oosik in Inuit), which can reach around one meter in length! For the last thirty years, a significant trade in fossilized mammoth ivory and molars has developed, which remains unregulated at the moment and which produces remarkable results. The most beautiful comes from the Siberian permafrost, but it can also be found in the North Sea, which requires stabilization. Semi-precious stones and mother-of-pearl also make wonderful decorative items.

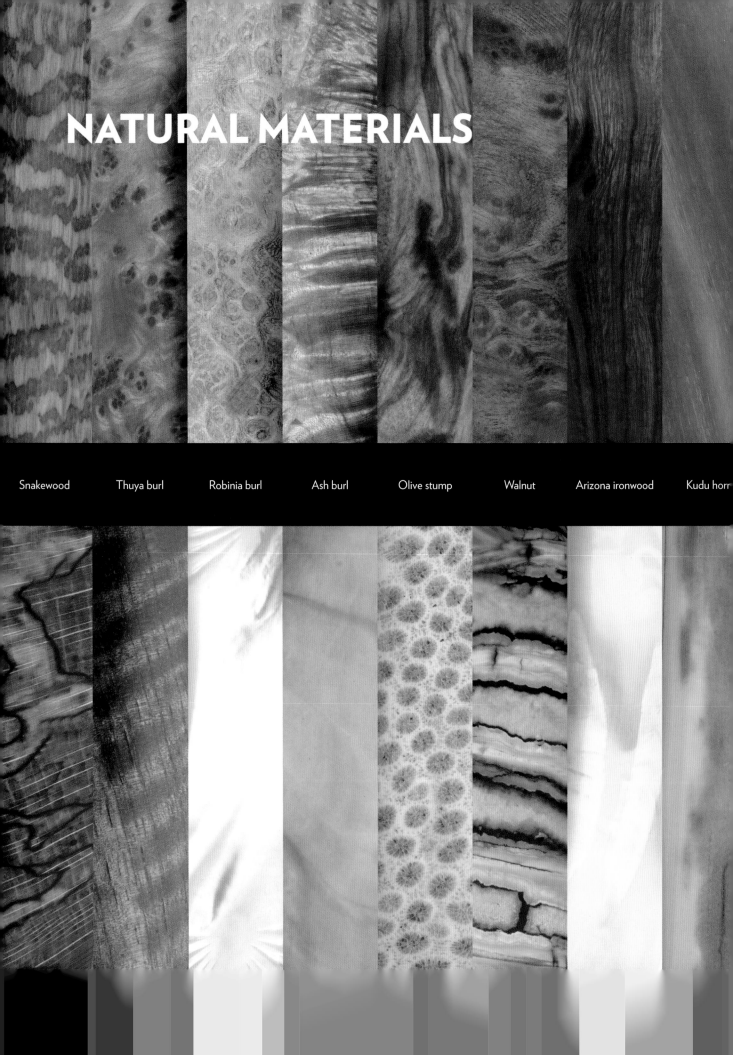

NATURAL MATERIALS

Snakewood   Thuya burl   Robinia burl   Ash burl   Olive stump   Walnut   Arizona ironwood   Kudu horr

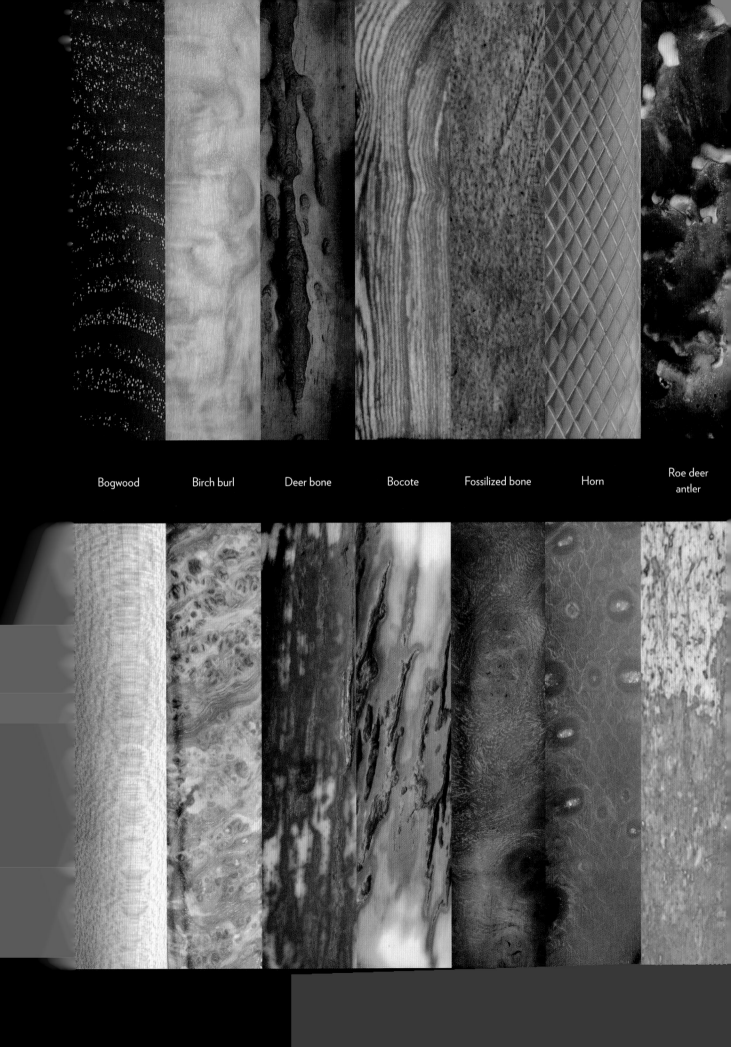

Bogwood   Birch burl   Deer bone   Bocote   Fossilized bone   Horn   Roe deer antler

COMPOSITE MATERIALS FROM MANUFACTURING

If we look back to the late 1970s, it is easy to see the veritable revolution that has since taken place in the knifemaking world, both in terms of the steels used for blades and the materials used to make handles. It is the latter that we are interested in here! If "boredom once came from uniformity", this is no longer the case today in the world of knifemaking.

PAPER STONE

First used in construction, this material is a mixture of recycled paper and a resin made from cashew tree shells — this is a tree that produces apples with a seed at the end, known as a cashew nut.

TEXALIUM

This is a material made from glass fiber with a thin aluminum layer covering its surface. The aluminum used on the surface is 99.99% pure and measures around 200 angströms thick (an angström is one ten-billionth of a meter).

JUMA®

Polyurethane-based material, which has excellent machinability (piercing, milling, grinding and polishing), with a low risk of breakage due to its uniform composition. It is thermoformable (in boiling water).

ELFORYN®

This is a material which imitates ivory, obtained by combining different minerals with a light-stable resin. It is non-yellowing.

MICARTA

This synthetic material, popularized by Bob Loveless in the 1970s (Micarta was originally a brand created by George Westinghouse at the very beginning of the 20th century), quickly enjoyed great success among American knifemakers, before becoming more widely used by manufacturers and artisans around the globe. It is a composite material obtained by compressing paper or other materials under high pressure (woven or not, rough cloth or loose rags, etc.) and a polymerized phenolic resin. It is resistant to water, many solvents, heat (not fire) and cold. It's easy to use, cuts easily, and can be sandblasted or polished. A great classic in the world of knifemaking.

G10

Made from a thin glass cloth saturated with epoxy resin, which may be stained or unstained. This material is very strong and easy to machine or sand. There is an almost infinite range of colors (even phosphorescent G10).

RIBBED ACRYLIC

Acrylic resin (PMMA) producing a colorful effect, quite rock 'n' roll!

CARBON FIBER

A product of the aviation and automobile industry, this revolutionary material is made of extremely fine fibers containing mainly carbon atoms (graphite). These are arranged in microscopic crystals which are positioned more or less parallel to the longitudinal axis of the fiber. The alignment of these crystals makes the fiber extremely tough for its size. Several thousand carbon fibers are wrapped together to form a thread, which can then be used as it is or woven.

This material is characterized by its low density (1.7 to 1.9), its high tensile and compressive strength, its flexibility, its good electrical and thermal conductivity, and its chemical inertia (except to oxidization). The material can be dyed in bulk (carbonwaves.com).

RECONSTITUTED STONES

A combination of crushed stone and resin. 70% mineral materials.

OTHER

There are other materials which are more widely used in the knifemaking industry than by artisans, such as FRN and GFN, made from fiberglass and nylon.

Orange G10 | Micarta | Carbon fiber | Texalium | Juma® cream

Black G10 | Carbon fiber and bronze wire | Ribbed acrylic | Reconstituted stone | Brown Micarta

STABILIZATION

Stabilization is the process of resin saturation (stained or natural) using a vacuum pump, of the core of a natural material, of animal, plant or mineral origin, which is fairly hard. This produces excellent results with wood in particular.

STABILIZED WOOD

The Mercorne company is a specialist in this area and distributes its products internationally. Stabilized wood provides the richness of wood with the strength of a polymerized resin. Therefore, you get a material with all the aesthetic qualities of natural wood without any of the drawbacks (deterioration due to external factors - humidity, temperature variation, etc.). Apart from the substantial improvements to the mechanical qualities of wood, this process presents the aesthetics in a remarkable way (iridescence, burls, forks, imperfections, etc.). Stabilization allows the characteristics in "poor" woods to be optimized. These woods are very soft and would otherwise be of no use for knifemaking, such as poplar wood.

OTHER STABILIZED MATERIALS

The process of stabilization by resin impregnation can also be used for materials which have become spongy and brittle due to long periods of exposure to sea water, ice or permafrost, such as mammoth and cetacean bones, mammoth or walrus ivory (or the remnants after cutting), corals, mammoth molars, spongy bones from various animals, etc.

GARY HEADRICK (USA)
folding knife with stabilized coral scales, Damascus steel blade and mokume-gane bolster.

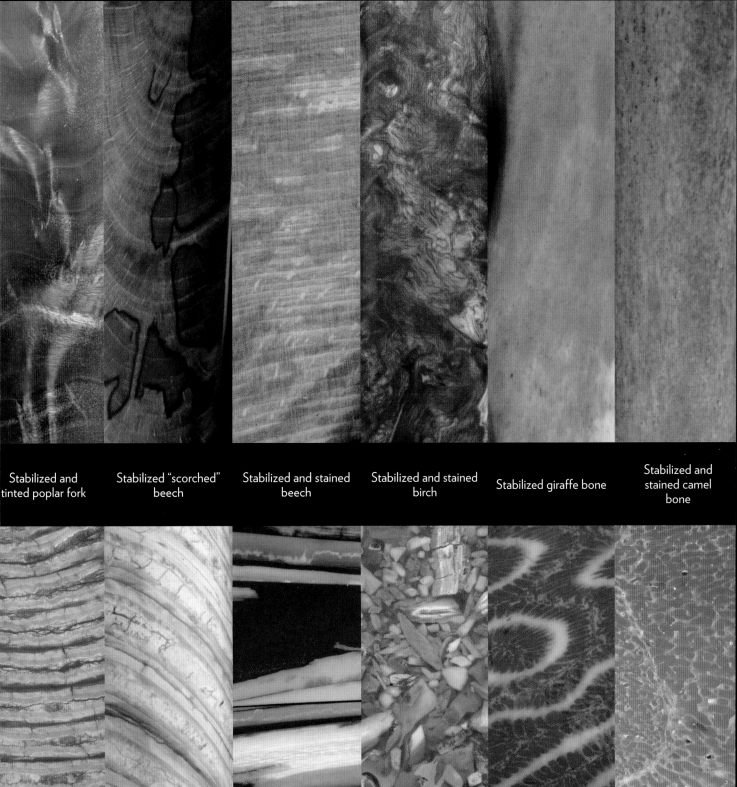

Stabilized and tinted poplar fork

Stabilized "scorched" beech

Stabilized and stained beech

Stabilized and stained birch

Stabilized giraffe bone

Stabilized and stained camel bone

Stabilized and dyed mammoth molar

Stabilized mammoth molar

Stabilized mammoth remnants

"Nougat" of stabilized mammoth ivory remnants

Stabilized fossilized coral

Stabilized fossilized coral

INCLUSIONS

In the 1950s, my father, an engineer by trade and sales representative in the chemical industry in Africa, taught one of his friends, a missionary in Gabon, the technique for incorporating exotic insects into polyester resin. Implementation was delicate and very strong-smelling. However, the idea took off and this type of inclusion could be found across large parts of French-Africa.

Today, acrylic resin has replaced polyester and allows a wide variety of often surprising inclusions: fabrics, feathers, paper, gold and silver leaf, pine cones, metal machining offcuts, various plants, and even cow dung from Aubrac (Mercorne)! It is only limited by human imagination. Acrylic is easy to work with, and it is cut with the same tools or machines as wood. It does not cope well with heat and must be handled delicately when being sanded or polished.

CRISTALIUM®

This material was originally designed by Tom Fleury and allows any type of product to be incorporated into acrylic glass, a genuine synthetic crystal called Cristalium®. A "smart" material with exceptional properties: it is clearer and glossier than glass, guaranteed to be non-yellowing, and both UV and solvent resistant.

THOMAS GONY (GRIND TACTICAL KNIVES)
"Tyrex" with carbon fiber scales and *Métapol* Spark (dovetail assembly), double grind blade. "Prickly" with digital camo G10 handle.

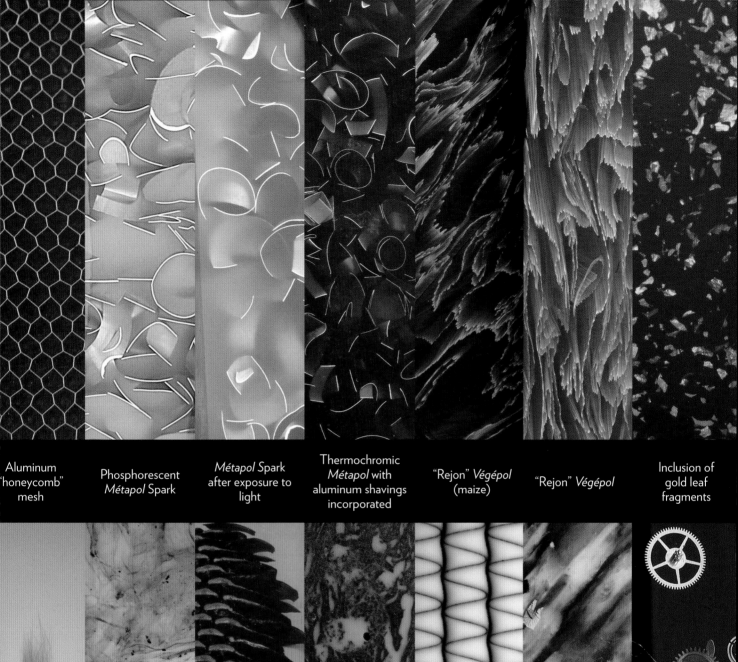

Aluminum "honeycomb" mesh

Phosphorescent *Métapol* Spark

Métapol Spark after exposure to light

Thermochromic *Métapol* with aluminum shavings incorporated

"Rejon" *Végépol* (maize)

"Rejon" *Végépol*

Inclusion of gold leaf fragments

Feathers and fishing fly inclusion

Reconstituted amber

Pine cone - resinated "pine nut"

Stabilized and stained cow dung

Cardboard packaging

Pounded magazines embedded in resin

Watch part inclusions in Cristalium©

FRANCK SOUVILLE (FRANCE)
Folding knife with multi-bar Damascus steel blade and mammoth ivory scales The "Sailor Jerry" carving is signed by Serge Raoux.

— ◆ —

KNIFE EMBELLISHMENT

SINCE THE BEGINNING OF TIME, ARTISTS HAVE SEARCHED FOR ALL SORTS OF MATERIALS WITH WHICH TO PRACTICE THEIR ART. WEAPONRY AND KNIFEMAKING PIECES HAVE PROVIDED INSPIRATION IN THE PAST, AND CONTEMPORARY KNIFEMAKING IS NO EXCEPTION TO THIS DESIRE FOR EMBELLISHMENT. SOME OF THESE TECHNIQUES FOCUS ON DECORATING THE METAL COMPONENTS — GUARD, POMMEL AND BLADE — WHILE OTHERS ARE LIMITED TO THE HANDLE.

— ◆ —

ENGRAVING AND CARVING

This technique consists of cutting metal with a sharp tool, harder than the metal being engraved. The engraver removes fine shavings following the outline of his design. This technique is called "intaglio": very little material is removed. Intaglio plays on shades of gray to create volume on the pattern to be engraved, unlike other goldsmithing techniques such as chasing which create significant relief by pushing the metal away.

The steel of the tools used for engraving is only slightly harder than the knife blades. It is fairly difficult to engrave the blade unless it is done during the knife manufacturing process, using heated steel, before quenching. The materials used for the handle and bolsters are usually much softer and it is mainly on these parts that the engravers practice their art.

The engraver's main tools are burins, hammers, chisels, sharpening stones and an engraver's vice.

The tip of the burin often resembles a "V" with a 90° angle whose face is ground at 50° or 60°. The engraver's hammer has a steel head weighing around 150 grams, the peen of is rounded and slightly domed. Another family of tools used is chisels. The cutting tool, with a very similar shaped tip to that of the burin, measures around 10 cm and it has mushroom-shaped wooden handle. With these tools, it is the pressure applied by the right hand which causes the tool to penetrate the surface of the material and remove a shaving. When the engraver uses a rotating vice, the left hand helps the cutting by "pressing" the engraver's object into the tool. The combination of the action of both hands allows for great flexibility but the cutting pressure is weaker than with a hammer. These tools are used for fine cutting details and shading.

The engraver starts with contours and then focuses on the "deep grooves", to prevent any parts of the engraving from being too flat. The bottom can also be treated with a perloir, a tool which has a very fine point with a small depression. By hammering the bottom, the engraver creates small, slightly rounded adjacent rounds which give a beaded look. Finally, there is shading and eventually polishing and inlays.

CARLO CAVEDON (ITALY)

Titanium "Walkirie" frame lock on the body; Damascus steel clip and blade. Chisel engraving.

勇気

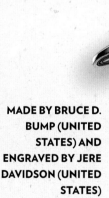

MADE BY BRUCE D. BUMP (UNITED STATES) AND ENGRAVED BY JERE DAVIDSON (UNITED STATES)

Bowie with an *amber stag* handle.

ALEXANDER GEVGALOV (BULGARIA)

"Samurai", an automatic folding mechanism, invented by Alex Gev (wedge lock). Gold, silver and copper inlays.

ETCHING

In use since the Middle Ages by Arab goldsmiths and many European artists (among which the most famous was Albrecht Dürer), acid etching was particularly widely used to decorate knives.

With the development of modern techniques which allow engravings to be done at a quality similar to photographs, this ancient art has almost been forgotten. Only a few artists, such as Spanish artist Antonio Montejano, have upheld its reputation with wonderful knifemaking creations.

Incorrectly called engraving, it is oxidization which produces excellent results on quenched and non-quenched steel, carbon and stainless steels, as well as copper. It is easy to procure the products and basic tools required. As for the technique, it is quite easy to master.

Originally, etching was done with pure or reduced nitric acid — which should be avoided, as it is highly corrosive and toxic. Today, iron(III) chloride is preferred (it should be noted that nitric acid does not damage stainless steels, unlike iron(III) chloride).

The process is very simple and divided into two different techniques. In negative engraving, the blade is completely covered in tar and the pattern is scratched with a needle. The parts which are then exposed are carved out with a sharp tool. With positive engraving, the pattern is painted onto the blade and remains exposed. The blade will be completely oxidized and the protected parts will give a relief engraving.

The prepared blade is then quenched in iron(III) chloride.

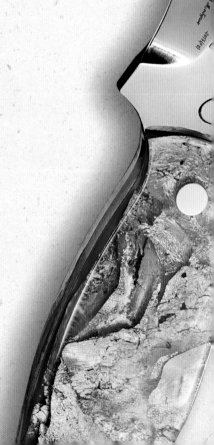

PAUL-EMMANUEL ARESTAN (FRANCE)
"Dragon" patterned blade, acid-etched.

DENIS MURA (ITALY)
Daggers acid-etched by the great expert in this field: Antonio Montejano (Spain).

SHEATH

These knives need a good outfit. This is a saddler's job as, generally, they are made from leather and beautiful skins: ray, ostrich, shark. Delicate or rustic, sheaths are generally made from naturally tanned leather (vegetable tanning). In a Nordic or Western style, simple or sophisticated: there's something for everyone.

Bertrand Montillet
A sheath being made.

A sheath made by saddler Bertrand Montillet, for a knife by Samuel Lurquin.

Bruno Dufort's carving method, to hold one of his knives.

CARVING

Sometimes folk art, sometimes mainstream art, depending on whether it is primitive or very elaborate, carvings have always decorated knife handles. As pictures demonstrate this better than words, here is a small selection.

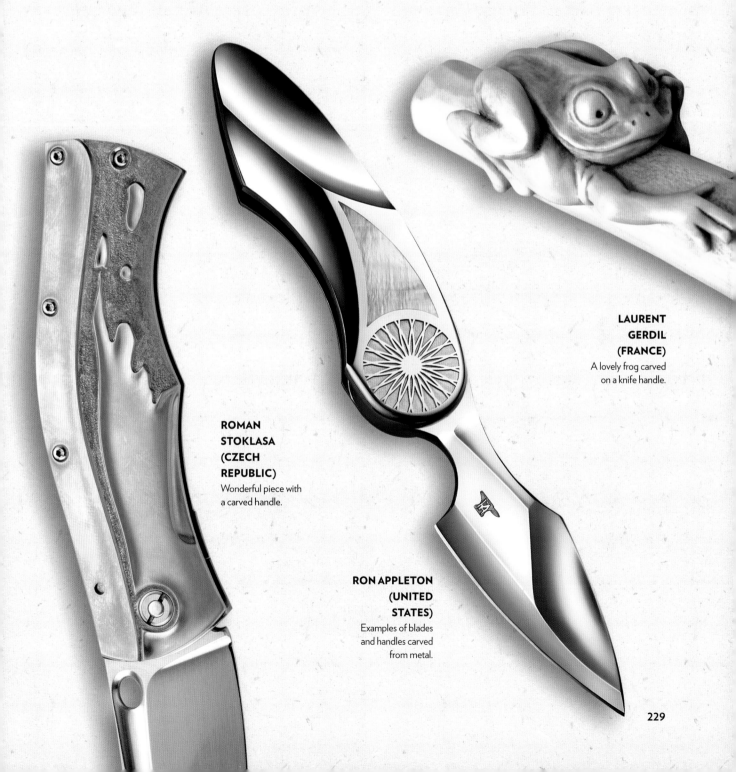

LAURENT GERDIL (FRANCE)
A lovely frog carved on a knife handle.

ROMAN STOKLASA (CZECH REPUBLIC)
Wonderful piece with a carved handle.

RON APPLETON (UNITED STATES)
Examples of blades and handles carved from metal.

229

SCRIMSHAW

We don't really know where the scrimshaw technique came from. It is an art form which consists of engraving the surface of a polished material and then applying ink that will remain in the grooves, dots, or lines, making the engraving stand out.

We are familiar with the scrimshaw work of the Inuits, but you should also be aware that we have found 13th century crossbows clad with ivory and covered with engraved hunting scenes. We have also found engraved bones or antlers in almost all civilizations, including the most "primitive".

The word came from the Dutch "Skrim-shander", which means "he who lets himself live", referencing the long hours sailors spent engraving the teeth of sperm whales. Be that as it may, this art, which was likely some of the earliest art to be produced, has now earned its reputation and can be considered an art in its own right, especially when it is practiced by perfectionists such as those presented in this paragraph.

The most popular materials, both among scrimshanders (artists specialized in scrimshaw) and their customers, are the various ivories: elephant (extremely well regulated) and fossilized ivories such as mammoth or walrus. Warthog teeth are very easy to find but are often cracked.

You can also try using antlers or bone, but these materials are often the most difficult to work with as they are usually quite porous which makes them trickier to polish.

Buffalo horn is the ideal material to work with in white on black, and Quebecois kni-femaker Gaétan Beauchamp excels in this medium. There are also resinous or synthetic materials which can be used. Although they are much less aesthetically pleasing, they lend themselves to these types of elegant engravings: micarta is the best example. Whatever the material may be, it must be as highly polished as possible: the slightest scratch will make it difficult to see when working and will retain ink when finished, resulting in a "messy" scrimshaw.

GAÉTAN BEAUCHAMP (CANADA)
at work.

GRÉGORY DELAUNAY (FRANCE)
Modern and hyper realistic scrimshaw being made.

GRÉGORY DELAUNAY (FRANCE)
Eurasian blue tit on a knife by André Thorburn (South Africa).

NATALIA ZABELINA (RUSSIA)
"Iris" with a san mai blade (mosaic Damascus). The handle is a copy of a Japanese engraving on walrus bone. Liner lock system.

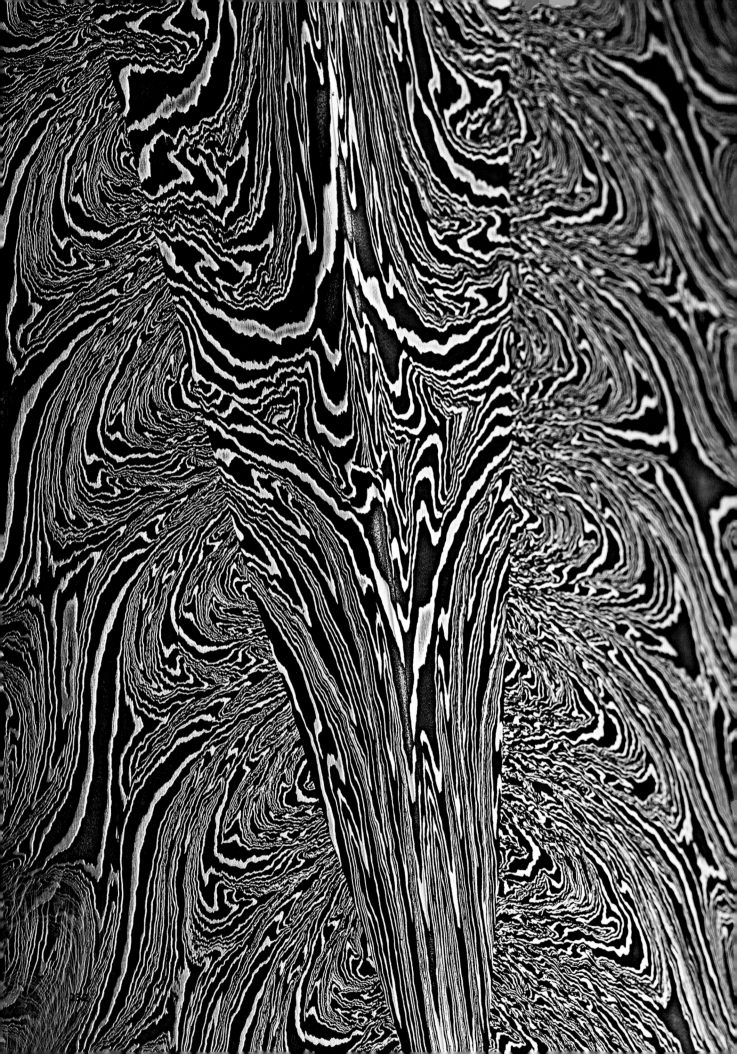

THE ROADS TO DAMASCUS

ITS NAME PROBABLY COMES FROM THE CAPITAL OF MODERN DAY SYRIA, WHERE THE CRUSADERS FIRST DISCOVERED IT. MAINLY SOLD IN THE CITY SOUKS IN THE FORM OF INGOTS OR VARIOUS SWORDS, THE STEEL PROBABLY CAME FROM INDIA OR PERSIA, HEADED FOR MIDDLE EASTERN MARKETS.

This "Damascus" was actually a crucible steel, called wootz (in India) or bulat (in Russia and Persia). But the Damascus discussed in this book is a layered steel, obtained by welding layers of iron and steel together, like a puff pastry.

The Celts, the Greeks, the Etruscans and, later, the Merovingians and Vikings knew about layered Damascus and used it for the blades of their swords. Originally, they were made from layers of wrought iron, welded together, then folded over and stretched several times to achieve an iron plate. Then man learned to master steel and it became layers of iron and steel, which was much more effective. Occasionally, "iron" from meteorites, containing nickel, was used.

The Damascus technique fell into disuse in the 16th century, man having mastered steel, especially its heat treatment. Damascus reappeared in the 19th century, on the barrels of guns, thanks to its great mechanical qualities.

— ◆ —

FROM SIMPLE LAYERS TO COMPLEX DAMASCUS

A legendary steel if ever there was one, all varieties of Damascus steel continue to be a source of fascination. Today, Damascus steel is used in many creative fields, such as jewelry, watchmaking, sculpture, armory, goldsmithing... and knifemaking of course!

Making laminated Damascus is quite simple, for a seasoned blacksmith. It consists of preparing a "set" of three, five, or seven alternating layers of iron and steel, which is then heated and welded in forge fire using a hammer or drop hammer. The resultant bar is cut and then folded, and then the process is repeated, with or without the addition of a welding agent (usually borax). If you start with seven layers, you will get 14, then 28, 56, 112, 224, 448, etc.

This bar can be used to make a blade which, when immersed in a solution of nitric acid or, even better, iron perchloride (some people even use diluted instant coffee), will take on this characteristic iridescent appearance, with the acid affecting different steels in different ways. The best contrasting effect is obtained using steels that have a high carbon content and steels with a small amount of nickel. This is layered Damascus, in its "simplest" form.

You can also twist, weld, chop and split Damascus steel to get as many different patterns as the blacksmith's imagination will allow.

Some of them are cut with digitally controlled wire machines (electrical discharge machines) and produce realistic patterns which are integrated into their Damascus (they are more or less shaped by forging). Others produce patterns on their sides which are then welded together in a repetitive way: this is "poetic Damascus" (as used by French blacksmith Pierre Reverdy), or mosaic Damascus.

Detailed look at the mosaic Damascus produced by Swedish blacksmith Mattias Styrefors: what amazing animal images!

1 2 French specialist Claude Schosseler, starting production on a Damascus steel bar.

3 Creating twisted Damascus steel.

4 Laminating a Damascus steel bar.

5 Patterns created by David Brenière.

His name is Persson, Conny Persson. He is Swedish.

Blades in heat-colored Damascus steel made by Swedish blacksmith Johann Gustafsson.

"Le Lien" (The Link), "poetic" Damascus steel blade by Pierre Reverdy.

236

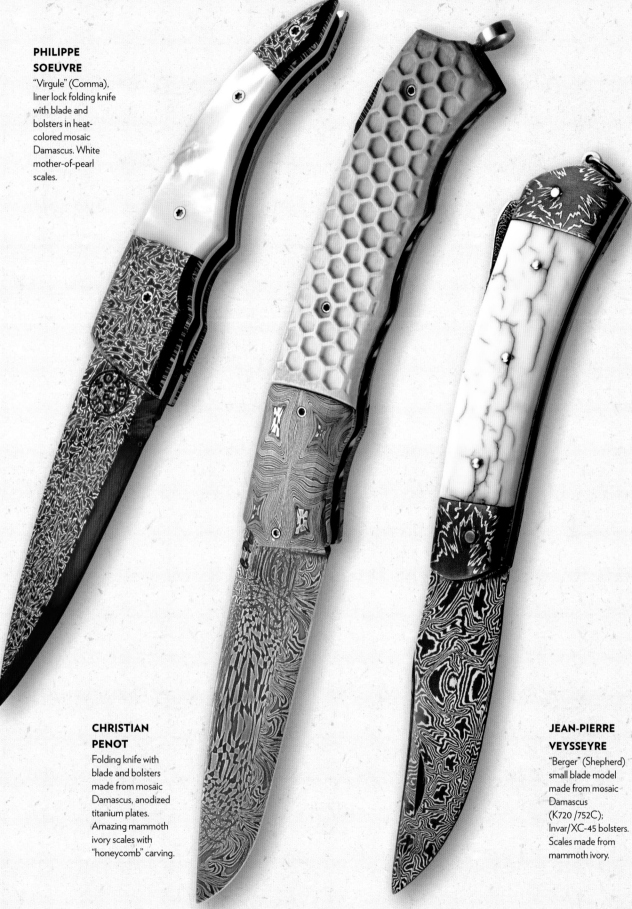

PHILIPPE SOEUVRE

"Virgule" (Comma), liner lock folding knife with blade and bolsters in heat-colored mosaic Damascus. White mother-of-pearl scales.

CHRISTIAN PENOT

Folding knife with blade and bolsters made from mosaic Damascus, anodized titanium plates. Amazing mammoth ivory scales with "honeycomb" carving.

JEAN-PIERRE VEYSSEYRE

"Berger" (Shepherd) small blade model made from mosaic Damascus (K720 /752C); Invar/XC-45 bolsters. Scales made from mammoth ivory.

GLOSSARY

B

Backstand: an essential machine for knifemaking.

Base plate: part of a fixed blade knife, in the length of the blade, on which the guard, scales and/or pommel are attached. This is known as base plate assembly.

Bolster: Two-part component attached on both sides of the handle on folding knives. One bolster, at the top of the handle; two bolsters, at the head and "butt" of the handle; three bolsters, if there is a central bolster.

C

Carbon (C): an essential element in steel composition. In knifemaking, we use the term "carbon steel", as opposed to stainless steel.

Choil: demarcation line on the blade, between the grind and the heel.

D

Damascus (steel): there is a chapter of this book dedicated to it. It can be oxidizable or stainless steel, depending on the materials used in its composition.

Ductility: the ability of a material to be synthetically shaped without breaking and, by extension, the flexibility of a blade.

E

EDC: an acronym for Every Day Carry. This is a commonly used expression for the design of a folding knife that might be used on a daily basis.

Edge: the cutting edge of the blade.

F

Ferrule locking system: this is the system made famous by Opinel.

Fly: the tip of the spring on certain folding knives (such as the Laguiole, known for its bee).

Forged: in the world of knifemaking, this is the term used for a knife whose blade has been heated in a forge, then shaped by hammering on an anvil or with a drop hammer. In contrast, a blade can be machined on a grinding wheel or a band grinder (backstand).

Frame lock system: derived from the liner lock, but more robust and made by using the handle's lock-plate (steel or titanium). Also called the "Chris Reeve lock", after its inventor.

Friction system: no blade retention.

Front-lock, mid-lock, and back lock locking systems: locking and unlocking the blade using a lever.

G

Grind: part of the blade which forms the cutting edge. It can be flat (V-shaped), concave, convex or even unilateral, as with scissors or Japanese cooking knives.

Guard: the part located between the blade and the handle, preventing your hand from sliding down the blade.

Guilloché: engraved designs achieved by removing metal (with file, burin, or acid) on different parts of a knife (back of the blade and spring).

H

Heat treatment: different processes performed on the knife blade, reversing the effects of machining or forging (heating and standardization), then hardening it (quenching), and finally, making it more flexible (tempering).

I

Iron (Fe): the main component of steel.

L

Liner lock system: once the blade is extended, a rod locks it in place. This steel or titanium rod must be moved to close the knife.

M

Micarta: composite material made of resin mixed with paper or cotton. Can be used to create highly resistant antibacterial knife handles.

Mokume-gane (Japanese term): layers of copper and brass, silver or gold, welded together via hot forging.

P

Palanquille: lever on the front of the spring of a folding knife, locking the blade.

Plates: parts of the handle on a folding knife. They are usually made of steel or titanium and can be covered with scales.

Q

Quenching: a process which consists of heating a piece of steel to a certain temperature (it varies based on the type of steel) and quickly cooling it by immersing it in a liquid (water, oil, salt bath) or in air, resulting in a hard structure known as martensite. At this stage, the steel is very hard but very brittle.

R

Resilience: resistance to impact.

Rivet: a small metal rod used, among other things, to attach scales and bolsters to the handle.

Rockwell (HRC): scale which measures the hardness of a blade. For knife blades, the HRC index is usually between 52 and 67 HRC.

S

Scales: parts, which generally come as a pair, attached to either side of the base or plates of the knife. They can be made from natural or synthetic materials.

Shagreen: tanned skin from certain varieties of sharks or rays.

Sharpen, hone, whet: processes designed to restore the "edge" or sharpness of a knife blade. This process is generally performed using a natural or synthetic sharpening stone or a steel or ceramic sharpening steel.

Slipjoint system: blade retention system, using a dorsal spring, but without locking it.

Steel: alloy composed mainly of iron and a low percentage of carbon (0.3% to 2%). It can be composed of different alloys, chromium in particular which, above 14%, gives it a good resistance to oxidization. The most commonly used steels for knifemaking are C75 (oxidizable), D2 (semi-oxidizable) and stainless steels: ATS-34, 440C, VG10, CPM S30V (powder metallurgy).

Swedge: a groove carved into the blade of certain folding knives in which a fingernail can be placed to facilitate opening.

System: a term used mainly for folding knives, which refers to the blade's method of folding and/or locking.

T

Tang: tapered length of the blade, which goes into the handle on fixed blade knives. This is known as tang assembly.

Tempering: a process that consists of heating a previously quenched part to a temperature lower than the quenching temperature (varies depending on the type of steel, generally between 200 °C and 400 °C). Tempering eliminates the brittleness of the steel and makes it stronger, while making it possible to adjust the desired hardness (expressed using the Rockwell scale) for the steel part.

In French:

La métallurgie artisanale. By Mayn Séry and Christian Moretti. Éditions Vial

Art et techniques de la forge. By Havard Bergland. Éditions Vial

Couteaux pliants de métiers. By Pierre-Yves Javel. Éditions De Borée

Catalogue du Forum International du Couteau Contemporain (FICX)

Les aciers damassés, du fer primitif aux aciers modernes. By Madeleine Durand-Charre. Éditions Mines Paris

In English:

Sheffield Exhibition Knives. By Bill Claussen and Bill Adams

Knives 2020. By Joe Kertzman

Trade magazines:

La Passion des Couteaux (quarterly) – www.lapassiondescouteaux.fr

Panorama Mondial de la Coutellerie - Annual special edition of La Passion des Couteaux

Excalibur. Quarterly

Trade shows dedicated to the art of knifemaking:

Coutellia: Festival International du Couteau d'Art et de Tradition. Thiers (63300). In May. www.coutellia.fr

Fête du Couteau. In Nontron, Périgord (24300). First weekend of August. www.facebook.com/feteducouteaunontron/

Forum International du Couteau Contemporain (FICX). Carreau du Temple, Paris 75003. In September. www.ficxparis.com

SICAC. Espace Charenton, Paris 75012. In September.

Salon du Couteau et des Arts de la Table (SCAT). Espace Jean Couty, Lyon (69009). In November.

CIC Show. Milan Marriott Hotel, Milan (Italy). In December. www.corporazioneitalianacoltellinai.com

WEBSITES

French topic forums:

www.forgefr.com: a forum mainly dedicated to forging and metallurgy.

www.forum.neoczen.org: general knifemaking forum

Retail sites:

www.mercorne.fr: materials for knifemaking

www.bois52-3apl.fr: cut precious woods

www.mammothivorytrade.com: specialist in the sale of mammoth ivory

www.couteaux-courty.com: Parisian specialist in the sale of knives to collectors

www.kindal.fr: Parisian specialist in the sale of knives to collectors

www.coutellerie-champenoise.fr: beautiful knives, in Reims

www.lagrandecoutellerie.fr: table specialist

www.depdep.com: swords and knives

www.polycoutelier.com: knifemaker and goldsmith, in Lyon

IMAGE CREDITS